Managing Supplier Relationships

IT Infrastructure Library

Neville Greenhalgh

Central Computer and Telecommunications Agency

London: The Stationery Office

ISBN 0 11 330562 1
ISSN 0956 2591

For further information regarding this
publication and other CCTA products
please contact:
Library
CCTA
Roseberry Court
St Andrews Business Park
Norwich NR7 0HS
Tel. 01603 704930

This document has been produced using
procedures conforming to
BSI 5750 Part 1: 1987; ISO 9001:1987

Table of contents

Foreword

Welcome to the IT Infrastructure Library module on **Managing Supplier Relationships.**

In their respective areas the IT Infrastructure Library publications complement and provide more detail than the IS Guides.

The ethos behind the development of the IT Infrastructure Library is the recognition that organizations are becoming increasingly dependent on IT in order to satisfy their corporate aims and meet their business needs. This growing dependency leads to growing requirement for quality IT services. In this context quality means 'matched to business needs and user requirements as these evolve'.

This module is one of a series of codes of practice intended to facilitate the quality management of IT services and of the IT Infrastructure. (By IT Infrastructure, we mean organizations' computers and networks - hardware, software and computer related communications, upon which application systems and IT services are built and run). The codes of practice will assist organizations to provide quality IT services in the face of skill shortages, system complexity, rapid change, growing user expectations, current and future user requirements.

Underpinning the IT Infrastructure is the Environmental Infrastructure upon which it is built. Environmental topics are covered in separate sets of guides within the IT Infrastructure Library.

IT infrastructure management is a complex subject which for presentational and practical reasons has been broken down within the IT Infrastructure Library into a series of modules. A complete list of current and planned modules is available from the CCTA IT Infrastructure Management Services at the address given at the back of this module.

The structure of the module is, in essence:

* a **Management summary** aimed at senior managers (Directors of IT and above, typically down to Civil Service Grade 5), senior IT staff and, in some cases, users or office managers (typically Civil Service Grades 5 to 7)

* the main body of the text, aimed at IT middle management (typically grades 7 to HEO)

* technical detail in Annexes.

The module gives the main **guidance** in sections 3 to 5; explains the **benefits, costs and possible problems** in section 6, which may be of interest to senior staff; and provides information on **tools** (requirements and examples of real-life availability) in section 7.

CCTA is working with the IT industry to foster the development of software tools to underpin the guidance contained within the codes of practice (ie to make adherence to the module more practicable), and ultimately to automate functions.

If you have any comments on this or other modules, do please let us know. A **Comments sheet** is provided with every module. Alternatively you may wish to contact us directly using the reference point given in **Further information**.

Thank you. We hope you find this module useful.

Acknowledgement

The assistance of the following contributors is gratefully acknowledged:

Jill Williams (under contract to CCTA from Digital Equipment Co Ltd)

Steve Wyles (under contract to CCTA from PA Consulting Group).

1. Management Summary

1.1 Introduction

No organizations are completely free of the influence of suppliers and, for many, the achievement of business objectives may depend to a large extent on the performance of their suppliers. Where an organization is dependent upon the efficient and effective use of IT to support its business, it is essential that it has good relationships with its suppliers of IT products and associated services. Suppliers in the context of this module are regarded as being external to the customer organization.

Irrespective of the size of a customer or supplier organization or whether relationships are formal and contractual or informal, the effective management of relationships is vital if customers are to make the right choices and get the best value from their investment in IT. If there is a good relationship, a contract, once agreed, should assume the role of a reference document. However, it is important that a contract clearly defines what is to be supplied, when, how, at what price and the allocation of responsibilities. The module refers to the role of a contract in a relationship but does not cover contractual issues in any depth.

The module discusses the different types of relationships, the changing technical and operational environment and the impact that this can have, and the 'ownership' and management of relationships.

The formal project approach to establishing effective relationships referred to in this module will probably only be applicable in large organizations but the guidance can be tailored according to circumstances.

1.2 What relationships?

The guidance in this module is primarily aimed at establishing effective relationships between internal IT service providers within an organization and the external suppliers of IT products and/or services which support or form part of the provided services. However, much of the advice is of value in any relationship between a customer and a supplier.

The increase in contracting out of IT service provision (possibly as a result of market testing exercises) means that organizations are becoming more dependent, with the associated risks, on external suppliers for the totality of their IT service provision. The effective management of supplier relationships in this situation is equally important, and the guidance in this module will also be relevant to internal business managers who are having to take on responsibility for controlling the quality of IT services provided by an external supplier.

1.3 Where to start to improve

To ensure that relationships with suppliers are effective and worthwhile an organization first needs to set clear objectives for these relationships which take account of the future direction and policies concerning IT services as set out in their IS strategy. Existing 'formal' relationships with suppliers, and the internal administrative procedures that support these relationships, should be evaluated to determine how effective they are.

Formal relationships need to be planned, maintained and regularly reviewed if resources are to be used efficiently and effectively. Informal relationships are also important but need not be controlled to the same extent.

Relationships in general are likely to be more effective when there are fewer contact points to maintain. Organizations should review the number and frequency of their contacts with a view to reducing them to a minimum and ensuring that the communication paths within each organization are effective.

Measuring the quality of a relationship between a customer and suppliers is largely subjective, but this is no surprise since relationships depend to a large extent on the skills and attitudes of the people involved to be successful. Unless the right type of people are given responsibility, poor relationships may result and the consequences can be significant in terms of loss of business efficiency.

The guidance in the module addresses all of the above issues involved in establishing effective relationships.

1.4 The role of the Supplier Manager

Most suppliers have Account Managers who have responsibility for designated customers, but customers rarely have similarly defined roles for dealing with suppliers. In order to improve any given relationship it is important that both customer and supplier have 'owners' of that relationship. This module recommends creating the role of a Supplier Manager in the customer organization who 'owns' a relationship with one or more suppliers on behalf of the customer. This will probably be a part-time role and in many cases it may be that an organization merely needs to formalize or reapportion responsibilities which existing staff already have.

A Supplier Manager has overall responsibility for ensuring the quality of relationships. However, managers of IT Services' functions, such as the Availability Manager and the Service Level Manager, still need to retain day to day management responsibility for certain aspects of supplier relationships or, with their staff, fulfil essential liaison roles. Senior management will also still have an important involvement in relationships, particularly those of a strategic nature. Where an organization has contracted out (outsourced) some or all of its IT service provision it may be more appropriate or necessary for the Supplier Manager to be in the business area rather than in the IT Directorate.

1.5 Benefits

The benefits realized from improving customer and supplier relationships can be highly significant in terms of quality of service and better value for money for both the IT Directorate and internal business customers. It also provides an opportunity for suppliers to gain a better understanding of customer needs.

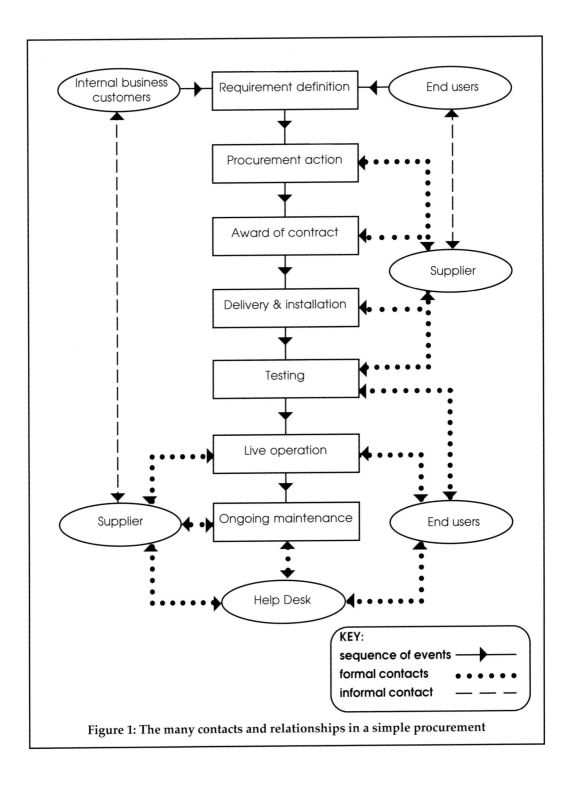

Figure 1: The many contacts and relationships in a simple procurement

2. Introduction

Often organizations pay insufficient attention to managing relationships with suppliers. The result is that neither customer nor supplier maximize the benefits they could realize from the relationship. Suppliers driven by the need to retain existing customers and obtain new business, tend to put more effort into fostering good relationships than their customers because their revenue may be affected. However it must always be remembered that a relationship involves a two way responsibility and customers who work at relationships will also reap benefits.

The interfaces between a customer and its suppliers are many and varied. Even a relatively simple purchase of hardware such as a mini computer, can generate a number of contacts with suppliers as the sequence of events passes from identification of the requirement, through procurement, to delivery, installation, testing, operation and maintenance. This is illustrated in Figure 1, opposite.

Both the customer and the supplier want to gain maximum benefit from their dealings with each other and it is easier to move towards this 'win-win' situation if good working relationships are fostered and properly managed. How often are remarks heard from customers like:

"They don't understand anything about the impact of this system on our business, they just sell boxes"; or

"We were suddenly faced with having to decide either to pay a 200% increase in maintenance charges or to hurriedly seek alternative options."

Conversely a supplier will make a commercial decision to bid a price to win a contract, but if in negotiations the customer succeeds in pressing the supplier to the limit on price, this may have a potentially damaging impact upon the customer and supplier relationship and be counter-productive in the long-term.

IT services have traditionally been supplied by internal providers. However there is now an increasing trend in organizations, in both the public and private sector, to contract out to external sources for provision of all or part of their IT services.

As part of the Government's Citizens' Charter initiative, the White Paper 'Competing for Quality' is aimed at improving the value of public services through competition. IT service provision is one of many areas within central government which is being 'market tested' to ensure that the internal service is compared with alternative sources of supply on an effectiveness and value for money basis. Whether market testing results in IT services continuing to be provided internally, or by an external contractor, having successful relationships with suppliers remains an important factor.

2.1 Purpose

The purpose of this module of the IT Infrastructure Library is to:

* help develop an understanding of the different types of customer and supplier relationships

* help organizations understand that better customer and supplier relationships will enable them to meet their business needs more effectively

* provide guidance on how to plan and implement efficient, cost-effective management of the relationships

* detail the benefits and possible problems of implementing better customer and supplier relationships

* explain how managing supplier relationships relates to other roles within IT service management.

2.2 Target Readership

This module is aimed at IT Directors, IT Services Managers and managers of IT Services functions such as availability management, computer operations management, Help Desk and service level management.

The module will also be of interest to any person within an organization who is involved in a customer and supplier relationship such as *intelligent customers*, senior business managers and procurement officers, and to the suppliers of IT products and services.

2.3 Scope

2.3.1 In the context of the IT Infrastructure Library

There are two modules in the IT Infrastructure Library which concentrate on relationships - this module and the **Customer Liaison** module.

The guidance in this module concentrates on relationships between an IT service provider (IT Services) within an organization and external suppliers of IT products and services. However it also takes cognizance of the increasing trend for IT service provision to be contracted out, whereby external suppliers are also the IT service providers and their relationship is then with the internal business customers within an organization. It explains how business managers in this situation, and in the situation where they are taking over responsibility for IT budgets, are having to take on more responsibility for specifying and managing their IS/IT and need to become intelligent customers. The module also provides useful generic guidance on relationships between customers and suppliers.

The Customer Liaison module covers relationships within an organization between an internal IT service provider (IT Services) and its internal business customers.

These relationships are shown in Figure 2. It is assumed in this illustration that the IT service provider is in-house.

The **Managing Facilities Management** module provides guidance on managing a specific relationship, that between an organization and a Facilities Management supplier.

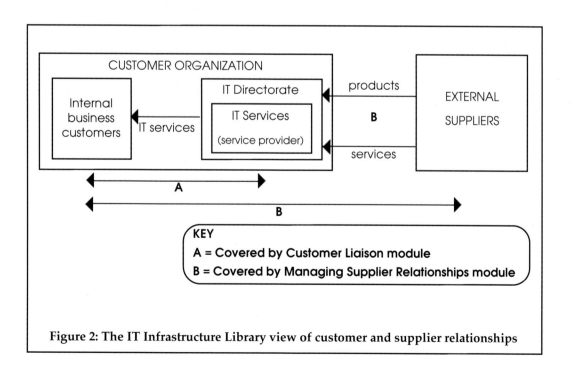

Figure 2: The IT Infrastructure Library view of customer and supplier relationships

**2.3.2 Outline of the
module**

The module focuses on managing relationships and not
contracts, although in many cases there will be one or more
contracts which form part of any given relationship. It
refers to different types of relationships but the guidance is
primarily aimed at managing long-term relationships more
effectively. Section 3.0 sets the scene by describing the
environment in which customer and supplier relationships
operate. It explains the different types of supplier, types of
relationships, the changing customer environment, the
changing technical and operational environment and
constraints on public sector organizations.

The module provides guidance on:

* planning to improve and establish effective customer
and supplier relationships by

 - carrying out an initial investigation/feasibility
 study (3.1.2 -3.1.9)

 - reviewing existing relationships (3.1.7) and
 examining what constitutes a 'good relationship'
 and a 'good contract' (Annex B) and how to
 assess the health of existing relationships
 (Annex C)

 - examining customer roles and responsibilities
 relating to relationships with suppliers (3.1.7,
 3.1.13, Annex D)

 - planning and developing revised procedures and
 practices for on-going and future relationships
 (3.1.11 -3.1.14)

 - planning to review relationships and contracts
 (3.1.15)

* building and managing more effective relationships
(Section 4)

* how to monitor relationships to ensure that they
remain healthy and effective (Section 5)

* the costs, benefits and problems associated with
improving relationships (Section 6).

2.3.3 The people factor

In a relationship between a customer and a supplier, by far the major responsibility for ensuring the success or failure of that relationship rests with the people involved. The module discusses the roles and responsibilities of personnel involved in these relationships (see Section 3.3 & Annex D).

2.4 Related guidance

This module is one of a series that constitutes the CCTA IT Infrastructure Library. Although the module can be read in isolation, it is recommended that it is used in conjunction with other modules.

The following modules provide guidance on IT service management functions where it is important that the manager, and often the staff of these functions, have a good working relationship with suppliers. Whilst this module provides some general guidance on managing those relationships, the individual modules should be referred to for detailed advice on managing the functions.

Availability Management

Capacity Management

Change Management

Computer Operations Management

Contingency Planning

Management of Local Processors and Terminals

Network Services Management

Problem Management

Service Level Management

Testing an IT Service for Operational Use.

Annex D explains how the roles and responsibilities of the managers of these functions relate to the customer and supplier interface.

The following other modules have some relevance to managing supplier relationships.

Configuration Management

Outlines how configuration management helps to control hardware and software assets, manage changes and handle incidents and problems. A configuration management database can provide information on the performance of suppliers' equipment, eg the number of incidents affecting an item, and contributes to the effective management of suppliers.

Managing Facilities Management	When an organization decides to contract out all or part of its IT service provision to an FM provider, this module gives guidance on the technical and administrative considerations in planning for, and managing, an FM contract and on the importance of setting up a Service Control Team (SCT) to manage the relationship with the FM provider.
Planning and Control for IT Services	Provides a framework for the planning and control activities required for effective service provision. The technical knowledge and future plans of suppliers should be used and taken into account in the planning and control of an organization's IT service provision.
Third Party and Single Source Maintenance	Gives guidance on the planning and management of single source maintenance contracts. If an organization decides to contract out the maintenance of all its computer equipment to a single source, then the relationship with that maintainer has a particular significance.

2.5 Standards

ISO 9001/EN 29001/BS 5750 Part 1 - Quality Management and Quality Assurance Standards

The IT Infrastructure Library modules are being designed to assist adherents to obtain third-party quality certification to ISO 9001. Such third-parties should be accredited by the NACCB, the National Accreditation Council for Certification Bodies.

PRINCE

This is the recommended standard project management method used in government departments.

ISEB Certificate in Service Management

The Information Systems Examination Board (ISEB) administers a proficiency-certification scheme for IT service management practitioners, including trainers and consultants.

3. Planning the management of supplier relationships

3.0 The supplier relationship environment

This sub-section describes the environment in which customer and supplier relationships operate. It is important to understand this environment before planning how to establish, improve and manage effective supplier relationships. The term environment is used loosely to cover the:

* various types of supplier in the market-place, giving information on the characteristics and motivation of each type (3.0.1)

* types of relationships, both purchasing and non-purchasing, which can exist (3.0.2)

* changing customer environment, ie the variations in the supply chain from end-user to supplier (3.0.3)

* changing technical and operational environments (3.0.4)

* constraints on public sector organizations (3.0.5).

The module uses various terms to describe those involved in relationships, such as supplier, customer, IT Directorate, IT Services, IT service provider, internal business customer and end-user. Their meaning within the context of this module is stated in the Glossary at Annex A.

3.0.1 Types of supplier

The types of suppliers are many and varied, however in general terms there are three main types:

* the commodity supplier

* the services supplier

* the Systems Integration supplier.

Whilst some large suppliers may be classed as all three types, and other suppliers may fall between these general types or move from one to another, the types are broadly representative of today's IT suppliers of products and services.

IT suppliers range from small retailers to multi-national corporations. They offer hardware, software and/or associated services, eg Facilities Management (FM), applications development, and consultancy.

With such a wide range of suppliers and services available it is important that an organization understands what it is looking for from its suppliers and selects the kind of supplier which can best meet its requirements now, and which is also likely to be able to do so in the future. For example, it would be wrong to expect a large training and support commitment from a supplier who is clearly selling commodity products and not services. It is also necessary to understand why a supplier wants to win a particular contract, it is rarely just to make a profit. It may be for example, for visibility in a particular market segment or to move in a new strategic direction. Understanding the supplier's capabilities and motives is an important stepping stone to establishing a good relationship.

3.0.1.1 The commodity supplier

The commodity supplier provides off-the-shelf products which can range from shrink wrapped software and relatively low cost PCs, to large value items of hardware. This type of supplier is geared to a low cost of sale and relatively short buying cycles. Some commodity suppliers may focus around a small product range while others will offer a large choice of products from many companies. The need to be competitive in the commodity market-place keeps prices down and profit margins on individual items are often low, therefore the commodity supplier is looking for high volume business to maintain profitability.

In addition, low margins mean that this type of supplier cannot usually afford to maintain a large support organization to provide pre- or post-sales support in a long procurement cycle. It is unlikely that customers will want to develop any lasting relationship with this type of supplier.

3.0.1.2 The services supplier

The services supplier provides personnel and services which are sometimes tailored to meet customers' needs. This type of supplier can range from a small organization providing only one type of service, eg training, to a large organization which is geared to provide a range of services, eg from project management to FM. Suppliers in this group range from consultancies through to FM suppliers and are generally heavily dependent on people to deliver the services. The quality and experience of supplier personnel will be of significant importance to customers when buying services. In many cases buying expertise is a costly exercise, therefore the services supplier has more flexibility with regard to pricing, and can invest more in the cost of sale, than the commodity supplier.

There is a large variety of different service providers, some of whom provide services based on their own systems and others who only have a limited investment in hardware or software on their own behalf. Some services suppliers may take a significant role in a consortium for a large project such as developing and implementing a major new system on a new hardware platform.

Typically this type of supplier provides a wide range of skills across most major hardware and software platforms. They are able to supply project management skills and consultancy on such wide-ranging topics as developing IS strategies through to software engineering.

3.0.1.3 The Systems Integration supplier

The main Systems Integration (SI) suppliers are large organizations, either a major manufacturer or a large services company, supplying an integrated set of both products and services as a complete solution, or with the role of integrating new and existing products from a range of suppliers. The SI supplier needs a good understanding of a broad range of technologies from a number of sources. Most SI suppliers will include products from a number of manufacturers and integrate them where this provides the most appropriate solution. However where they have their own products, they may still try to sell these in preference to competitors' products.

The large SI supplier has a large services organization designed to support the customer through every phase of a complex procurement and implementation. If there is a gap in the SI supplier's own capabilities, it is usually filled by alliances with third parties and the SI supplier is adept at managing consortia and picking the right partners to meet requirements. Large SI suppliers tend to be geared towards attracting relatively few, but high value, customers.

Some SI suppliers may specialize in smaller scale projects such as integrating specific application software on a range of PCs. Also where a services supplier is used to manage the service element of a multi-sourced procurement such as installation, project support and accommodation services etc, this is often referred to as a systems integration role which smaller companies often fulfil.

3.0.2   Types of relationship

The types of relationship possible with suppliers are affected by the size, complexity, and expected life, of what is to be supplied. They are also influenced by whether both supplier and customer hope to do business in the future, and how they have done so in the past.

It is important that customers have a clear idea, at the outset, of the nature of the relationship that they wish to establish, and that they set the expectations of the supplier accordingly. Some examples of typical customer and supplier relationships are given in Annex E.

Relationships can be split into two broad categories:

* purchasing

* non-purchasing.

3.0.2.1   Purchasing

Purchasing relationships are mostly contractual but also include purchasing arrangements between a customer and supplier which are likely to, but may not, lead to future contracts. Any purchase, from a supplier, is legally governed by a contract. The nature of the contract should reflect rather than define the relationship between supplier and purchaser.

Customers' purchasing relationships with suppliers have often varied between two extremes:

* a rather hostile contractual relationship with the customer seeking to invoke penalty clauses at an early stage

* long-term 'comfortable' associations with particular manufacturers often because of the customer's investment in that supplier's products.

A more enlightened approach to purchasing relationships is where the right balance is created between competition and obtaining best value for money over, for example, the life of a system, and the development of closer business working relationships with chosen suppliers. The contract however is still important (Annex B.2 explains what constitutes a 'good contract').

Purchasing relationships are many and varied but for
reference purposes they are divided into three general
categories:

* short-term

* medium-term

* long-term.

Short-term

Short-term relationships are those involved in, for example,
a one-off hardware or software procurement, or the
purchase of a training course. Whilst these purchases are
often important to customers, they usually involve limited
interactions with suppliers. The suppliers in this type of
relationship will, in the main, be commodity suppliers but
also include some service suppliers.

Medium-term

Medium-term relationships with suppliers may be covered
by a framework, or call-off contract, spanning two or three
years. This commits both parties to interact over a period
during which customer needs and the business
environment may change, and a more flexible relationship,
which can accommodate change, is therefore in the interests
of both parties.

The level of involvement for a supplier in this type of
relationship may be similar to the short term relationship
but over a longer period, or the circumstances may be such
that it is worthwhile to both parties to invest more resource
to ensure a successful relationship. These types of
relationships may evolve into longer term relationships.

Long-term

Long-term relationships, ie covering five years or more,
have always existed, for example with long-term
maintenance contracts, but some suppliers are now forming
what are generally known as *strategic partnerships* with large
clients, eg for software development work.

Long-term relationships require a shared deeper level of
knowledge of each other's organizational practices and
plans. A long-term supplier may be prepared to share
useful information to aid a customer's planning of long-
term strategies and how these might best achieve business
objectives.

This type of relationship needs trust and flexibility on the
part of both parties and an investment in terms of both
management and staff time to build the relationship and
make sure that it is understood. There are usually regular,
though not necessarily frequent, meetings at different
management levels to help progress the relationship.

Whilst the customer still needs to safeguard against being 'locked-in' to a particular supplier, this type of relationship can also bring real benefits. Customers may be given access to a wide range of skills and peripheral benefits. Suppliers can usually expect a continuing level of business, although for public sector organizations public sector purchasing policy and EC Directives still need to be observed.

3.0.2.2 Non-purchasing

Whilst most customer and supplier relationships are undoubtedly based upon a purchase or contract, there can be instances where relationships may exist without any purchase having taken place.

Exchange of information

The exchange of information and future plans between a customer and existing and potential suppliers, can benefit both parties. From the customer's point of view this type of relationship is invaluable in that:

* it helps them to keep abreast of changes in technology

* they can obtain advice on how to use their IT for competitive advantage

* they can discuss alternative approaches to the provision of services.

Suppliers benefit by influencing and elucidating existing and potential customers' future requirements and by keeping up to date with the market trends. The need to respect confidentiality may well be of prime importance in relation to the exchange of some information.

Relations between suppliers

In other circumstances a relationship may exist between two suppliers at the request of a customer. For example if the success of a project is heavily reliant on a number of suppliers, but each has a separate contract, a customer may wish to introduce a formal code of practice to ensure that suppliers work together effectively. This concept is often introduced by large organizations who have two or more strategic suppliers and wish to ensure continued compatibility in their strategies.

3.0.3 The changing customer environment

IT Services has traditionally had contractual relationships with external IT suppliers covering the maintenance of hardware and the provision of services to support its

Service Level Agreements (SLAs) with its internal customers. However, changes within customer organizations mean that new relationships with external suppliers are now also developing.

3.0.3.1   Traditional supply

Traditionally internal business managers defined the business requirements and the IT Directorate supplied the technical solutions. In this scenario IT Services:

* is a provider of IT services to its internal business customers, usually under the terms of one or more SLAs

* provides and maintains its level of service via purchases from suppliers or the placing of service contracts.

IT Services is the customer of, and maintains relationships with, external suppliers. There is usually only limited contact between internal business customers and suppliers. Figure 3 illustrates this situation and is an adaptation of Figure 2.

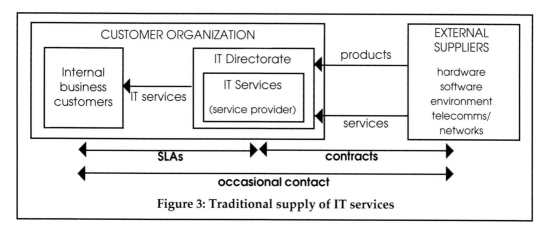

Figure 3: Traditional supply of IT services

Where IT Services have a charging policy and internal customers are actually charged (where internal business customers are the budget holders for IT service provision), or merely charged against a notional budget, this should not significantly affect IT Services' relationship with suppliers. However once internal business customers are being charged for services they may want to take a greater interest in service provision and therefore in relationships with suppliers (see 3.1.13.2).

3.0.3.2 IT Services as contract manager

The situation may arise where IT Services, in addition to the traditional situation explained at 3.0.3.1, is also a contract manager for internal business customers. This is often the case in framework contracts where an outline contract is established between a supplier and a customer's IT Services, supplemented by simpler arrangements directly between the internal business customer and the supplier. For example, the supply of PCs which are purchased as and when required by business customers, but under one framework contract negotiated by IT Services. In these circumstances IT Services has financial responsibility and accountability, polices the contract and gives purchasing and technical advice to the internal business customer. The supplier therefore has two relationships to maintain.

3.0.3.3 Facilities Management or contracting out

Organizations within both the public and private sector are increasingly concentrating on their core business activities and splitting off or contracting out their IT service provision. This is being achieved in two main ways:

*   by creating a separate company or Agency (within government departments) of part or all of the existing IT facility within an organization

*   by contracting out IT service provision to an external provider.

In the first situation the IT Directorate within a government department may become an Agency and sell its services back to its original parent department. Similar situations exist in the private sector where an organization's IT department may become a separate company.

The second situation is often referred to as Facilities Management (FM) or contracting out (outsourcing), where a decision is taken to use an external supplier to provide IT services.

An organization's requirements for FM or contracting out, can range from one aspect of IT services such as data preparation, through to total IT service provision. Indeed FM is often taken to mean the provision of an organization's complete infrastructure including building maintenance, provision of restaurant facilities and IT support, and the FM supplier may contract provision of some of these services to other suppliers.

For any contract with an external provider there might be a mix of ownership of assets between the provider and the customer organization. A common example is for the external provider to use their own, or purchase the customer's central computer systems and associated premises, and for the customer to retain ownership of distributed equipment, such as PCs, located in users' offices. There may be a mix of ownership and responsibility for maintenance of systems or application software.

Whoever owns the hardware, software, networks and environmental infrastructure, the future responsibility for administration of contracts and agreements for the supply of these products and services must be clearly stated in the contracts. Where the external provider is to be responsible, which is usual, the customer needs to be satisfied that any maintenance contracts and support agreements that are entered into by the external provider, with other suppliers, are adequate to support the level of service to which the external provider is contracted.

Service Control Team

Where an external provider is used, a Service Control Team (SCT) should be set up to manage the IT provider on behalf of the customer organization and to ensure the effective provision of IT services to the business. In this situation the SCT occupies a pivotal role in the relationship between the business and the external provider. The SCT helps to negotiate the contract with the external provider, and is responsible for the ongoing technical management of the contract which includes:

* monitoring the quality of delivered service post contract

* liaising with the external provider

* generally looking after the business customers' interests

* auditing the external provider's activities for compliance to the terms and conditions of the contract, including requirements to adhere to policies and standards

* negotiating the renewal or termination of the contract.

The SCT may reside within the IT Directorate if one still exists (ie if some aspects of IT are still carried out in-house such as applications development) or where there is no in-house IT capability it should be part of an intelligent customer function within an organization.

The intelligent customer function should be set up as a bridge between internal business customers and the provider(s) of IS/IT services. It needs to take on responsibility for managing the service provider(s) and to acquire the knowledge and seek advice (previously available from their own IT Services) to enable them to ensure that their information systems support the needs of the business efficiently and effectively. The intelligent customer function may be set up in individual business areas or there may be one function serving all business areas. For a brief definition of the intelligent customer function see the Glossary in Annex A. For more information on the intelligent customer see CCTA's Market Testing IS/IT booklet "The *Intelligent Customer*".

The **Managing Facilities Management** module of the IT Infrastructure Library gives detailed guidance on the plans and controls required by an organization to manage an FM provider and describes more fully the role of the SCT.

Figure 4 illustrates the situation where the SCT is part of an intelligent customer function within a business area in a customer organization and shows the relationship with the external service provider.

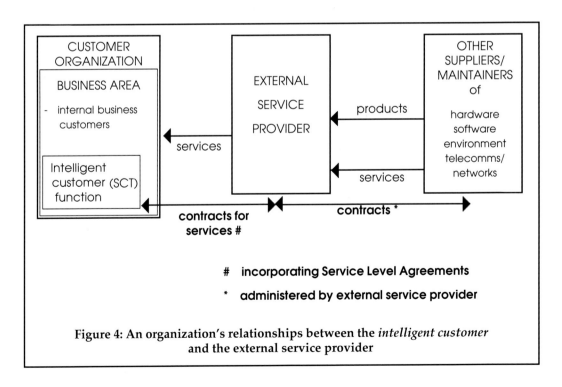

Figure 4: An organization's relationships between the *intelligent customer* and the external service provider

3.0.4 The changing technical and operational environment

The technical and operational environment within which customer and supplier relationships operate has been changing over recent years, with improvements in technology and the increasing need in the current economic climate for customers to have more flexibility in the use of their IT systems. The portability of IT solutions has therefore assumed increasing importance and organizations are moving from proprietary to open systems architectures and seeking to integrate systems from different suppliers. Having effective relationships with suppliers is particularly important for an organization which is changing its technical and operational environment, in order to help maintain an effective and efficient IT service to internal customers.

Single supplier/ single architecture

The single supplier and single architecture scenario, which is becoming increasingly rare, is the simplest relationship. Here a single supplier is providing a customer's complete IT architecture from its own product set. This requires no co-ordination with other suppliers.

Single supplier/ multiple architectures

A rather more involved situation arises where a single supplier is providing or supporting several architectures, ie different software environments, to meet a customer's requirements. Here the supplier has to take on a prime contractor role which inevitably involves them in additional risk and potentially leads to a more complex contract and the need for a more carefully managed customer and supplier relationship. The **Third Party and Single Source Maintenance** module of the IT Infrastructure Library provides guidance on the planning and management of single source maintenance contracts.

Multiple suppliers/ multiple architectures

Where a customer has multiple suppliers and a multi-architecture environment, the effort required to integrate applications is likely to be significant. The IT Directorate may wish to have a non-contractual code of practice between its suppliers to facilitate their working together effectively. This is obviously the most complex situation to manage and relies on a good relationship with all suppliers rather than the strength of any contract. However a nested approach can be adopted where one supplier assumes prime responsibility.

Maintenance contracts in a multi-supplier environment may need additional care in defining how to determine the performance of individual suppliers and the allocation of responsibility when problems occur.

Downsizing

Instead of applications being run on a mainframe-based system, they are increasingly being placed on smaller machines, such as PCs or mini workstations, which are usually connected by a network. This change in mode of operation is termed downsizing or rightsizing.

Downsizing often leads to a multi-supplier environment where there is a greater need for effective co-operation between suppliers and good relationships with the customer organization.

Increased complexity

The integration of multi-supplier systems and the increasing use of standards-based open systems, means that the purchase of systems and services is becoming more complex and requires a greater exchange of information between customer and supplier if the maximum value is to be obtained from the purchase. There is a greater, albeit more complex, range of options available to both suppliers and customers. Suppliers may know the possible alternatives better than the customer and may be able to provide innovative approaches to customer requirements, and it is important that best use is made of this knowledge. This is where a systems integrator supplier can be of benefit (see 3.0.1.3).

3.0.5 Constraints on public sector organizations

Public sector organizations do not have a completely free hand when it comes to selecting their suppliers and procuring IT products and/or services. A range of both purchasing and non-purchasing relationships are explained at Annex E but not all may be available as options in the public sector. In particular, long-term strategic relationships may be regarded as failing to meet EC and UK Government requirements for fair and open competition in IT procurements of goods and services.

Central government departments and other parts of the public sector are subject to the GATT Agreement on Government Procurement and EC Supplies Directives, the latter being implemented in the United Kingdom by means of the Public Supply Contracts Regulations 1991. The EC Services Directive, extends regulations to the procurement of services.

Purchasing organizations subject to the regulations regarding the supply of goods and services must currently:

* advertise most requirements which are over a certain value as competitive procurements in the EC Journal

* comply with regulations during the procurement process

* publish a notice of award of contract in the EC Journal.

There may also be a requirement on organizations to publicize their planned purchasing programme in the EC Journal. It is important that both customers and all potential suppliers are fully aware of the procedures being used in each procurement process. However as more public sector organizations contract out their IT service provision and transfer their assets to external suppliers, the above restrictions will no longer affect them.

3.1 Procedures

This section gives guidance on the planning required to examine and improve existing customer and supplier relationships and to establish effective new relationships. A project approach is adopted but setting up a formal project, using a project management method such as PRINCE, may only be appropriate in large organizations. Alternatively the initiative could be included as a sub-project within another wider project such as implementing a Quality Management system.

In smaller organizations a less formal approach may be more appropriate but most of the steps identified in Figure 5, overleaf, will still need to be carried out. The guidance is intended to be comprehensive and organizations should adapt it to suit their circumstances. However, any organization which has continuing relationships with suppliers should consider the need to improve them.

If a formal project is initiated it can be divided into three main phases:

* initial investigation/feasibility study (3.1.2 - 3.1.9)

* planning and development of revised practices and procedures, broken down into stages (3.1.10 - 3.1.16)

* implementation (Section 4).

A breakdown of these phases is shown at Figure 5.

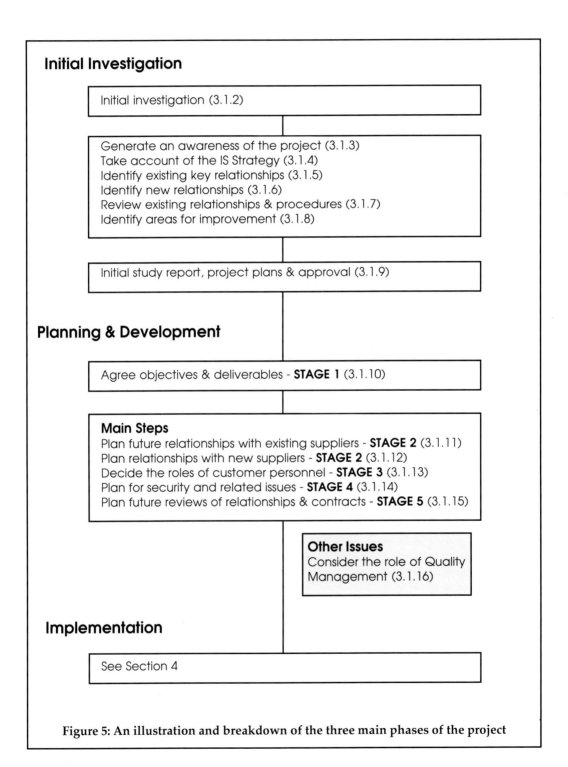

Initial Investigation

Initial investigation (3.1.2)

Generate an awareness of the project (3.1.3)
Take account of the IS Strategy (3.1.4)
Identify existing key relationships (3.1.5)
Identify new relationships (3.1.6)
Review existing relationships & procedures (3.1.7)
Identify areas for improvement (3.1.8)

Initial study report, project plans & approval (3.1.9)

Planning & Development

Agree objectives & deliverables - **STAGE 1** (3.1.10)

Main Steps
Plan future relationships with existing suppliers - **STAGE 2** (3.1.11)
Plan relationships with new suppliers - **STAGE 2** (3.1.12)
Decide the roles of customer personnel - **STAGE 3** (3.1.13)
Plan for security and related issues - **STAGE 4** (3.1.14)
Plan future reviews of relationships & contracts - **STAGE 5** (3.1.15)

Other Issues
Consider the role of Quality
Management (3.1.16)

Implementation

See Section 4

Figure 5: An illustration and breakdown of the three main phases of the project

A Project Board should be set up by the IT Director or senior business manager to provide overall guidance and to monitor the project's progress. The Project Board should agree the scope of the project in terms of which suppliers are to be included and the areas within the organization to be examined. The Board should appoint a project manager who will be responsible for:

* planning the project and defining individual responsibilities

* the day to day management of the project

* ensuring that the project progresses through to implementation to time and budget.

A person who is likely to take on the role of a Supplier Manager (see 3.1.11.1) would be an appropriate candidate for the role of project manager.

3.1.1 Aims and objectives

The overall aim of the project is to establish effective supplier relationships between an organization and its external suppliers.

High level objectives should be to:

* improve existing relationships

* identify if there are any unsatisfactory relationships

* identify new relationships required.

More specific objectives for the project are to:

* establish relationships with suppliers which are relevant to current and future business needs

* improve communications and ensure that contacts with suppliers are conducted in an efficient, honest and courteous manner

* define the 'ownership' of relationships

* establish which customer managers need to have, or to retain, a liaison or management role in relationships with suppliers

* obtain a clear understanding of which relationships with which suppliers are the most important in achieving business objectives

* identify potential benefits of improved relationships and reciprocal risks if no changes are made

* establish procedures for monitoring and reviewing the continuing effectiveness of supplier relationships.

Achievement of these objectives will help organizations to meet their business objectives through improved IT service provision. For instance, there should be fewer problems arising from the services provided by suppliers and those that do arise can be handled more effectively before they become serious. In addition, suppliers should gain an improved understanding of which issues are critical to an organization.

3.1.2 Initial investigation

Carry out an initial study to establish the relative importance of supplier relationships to the organization, and to examine current relationships and procedures to determine their effectiveness. Typical terms of reference for such a study could be to:

* generate an awareness of the project

* take account of the IS strategy in considering relationships

* identify key relationships and their role in achieving business objectives

* identify what new relationships may be required

* assess the effectiveness of existing relationships

* identify areas for improvement

* identify potential benefits of improved relationships

* produce a report covering the findings of the study and a project plan for improving existing and establishing effective new relationships.

3.1.3 Generate an awareness of the project

As the initial investigations will involve meeting a wide spectrum of staff and management it is important that some advance notice is given to them of the purpose of the initial study, what is involved and what contribution they will be expected to make.

This can be achieved by carrying out an awareness campaign involving one or more of the following:

* making preliminary visits to selected areas

* giving presentations to individual managers

* holding group seminars

* issuing leaflets or circulars.

The awareness campaign will need to be targeted at:

* IT Directorate personnel, in particular the managers of IT Services functions

* internal business customers

* both IT and internal business senior management

* relevant supplier personnel such as Account Managers and senior management.

At this stage it will only be possible to give information in general terms and there will be a need for further awareness initiatives during the development stage of the project.

3.1.4 Take account of the IS strategy

If an organization has an IS strategy it is important to take into account the policies defined in the strategy to ensure that:

* any impact on current and future relationships is properly evaluated

* the study is correctly focused and to prioritize the order in which relationships need to be examined.

The IS strategy will:

* identify the future business direction

* include a vision of how IS will support that future business direction

* translate that vision into a positive statement of the way forward in terms of information systems, information and organization and policies.

For example an organization's IS strategy may include policies, of relevance to supplier relationships, on:

* the implementation and use of IT standards

* the adoption of open systems

* suppliers being certified to ISO 9000/BS 5750 series of quality standards for their production process or maintenance procedures

* the implementation of security measures.

Examination of these policies may help to identify key relationships and probable new relationships. For further information on IS strategies see the CCTA Information Systems Guide **A2, Strategic Planning for Information Systems**.

3.1.5 Identify existing key relationships

It is necessary to identify existing key relationships, and determine where most advantage can be gained from improved supplier relationships. For example, if an organization has made a decision that a major business application is to continue running on a proprietary operating system for five more years, then the relationship with the supplier of that system will be of prime importance in maintaining a good service.

Another important factor in identifying key relationships is to understand the dependence on suppliers and to identify which services supported by a supplier have a major impact on achieving the business objectives of an organization. Establishing a good relationship with that supplier must have a high priority.

3.1.6 Identify new relationships

Having understood which current relationships are most important it is necessary to try and identify from the future business direction and plans of the organization, what new relationships might need to be pursued or developed. For example, if the need for considerable consultancy or project management expertise is foreseen over the next few years, then future relationships with one or more services suppliers could become of particular importance.

3.1.7 Review existing relationships and procedures

3.1.7.1 General

The process of planning effective customer and supplier relationships must include an assessment of the organization's current relationships with suppliers. It is also essential to establish how effective the customer organization is at currently managing relationships before attempting to move forward.

A purchasing and contracts section will have details of suppliers with whom contracts exist or these may be held on a database of contracts management information, which may be part of a Configuration Management Database.

When reviewing existing relationships take into account the views of any internal business customers involved in the relationships, as well as the suppliers, to try to ensure that an overall view is formed. There may be many factors which need to be taken into account when considering relationships. Guidance on what constitutes a 'good relationship' and a 'good contract', and what both a customer and supplier are looking for in a relationship, is given at Annex B.

The key relationships will have been identified and prioritized (see 3.1.5) and the next phase is to identify for each of the key relationships the associated risks and current success factors.

Examine risks

Examine the risks of not having a good relationship with a particular supplier. Understanding what can happen if the organization is let down, or if a supplier fails to grasp the importance of some critical requirement, is a good guide to identifying what aspects need to be monitored or improved in the relationship. For example, if an organization is reliant on a supplier for end-user support of a critical business application, an ineffective relationship could present a business risk.

Carry out a 'health check' of relationships

Carry out a 'health check' for each relationship. This involves asking a number of questions to gauge how successful they are at present. Use this not simply as an initial means of understanding the quality of a relationship, but also as a continuous check for improvement during the life of the relationship. Do not measure the success of the project against the quality of the relationships in absolute terms but in terms of improvement.

An example questionnaire is provided in Annex C, and the following sections describe the major aspects which need to be considered.

3.1.7.2 Review the relevance and effectiveness of existing relationships

Examine each existing relationship to ensure its relevance in the current situation. Determine how effectively each relationship is currently managed. It is important to ensure that time and energy spent on a relationship actually benefits the business. The interfaces which may exist between customer and supplier personnel are many and varied. The main interfaces are shown diagrammatically at Annex F.

Establish whether all the interfaces which are appropriate do exist, and whether existing relationships are meeting the declared objectives. For example:

* where it is of relevance to the relationship, do both customer and supplier appreciate each other's business objectives?

* are communications channels properly defined?

* are supplier personnel interfacing effectively with IT Services staff?

* are suppliers complying with the customer's change management system and using the correct channels to discuss changes?

* is there a good flow of information from strategic suppliers about future products to help a customer develop their IS strategy?

In many cases existing relationships will have happened by default rather than planning. It is necessary to check whether both parties understand their responsibilities within the relationship. It is also important to include existing relationships between customer's and supplier's senior management in the review.

3.1.7.3 Review existing contracts

Contracts with maintainers of IT infrastructure components should be being regularly reviewed to ensure that they enable IT Services to meet any SLA requirements. However during the review of existing relationships it is worth checking that the relevant people fully understand the obligations of both customer and supplier in the contracts.

3.1.7.4 Review existing roles and responsibilities

Examine who is currently managing the relationships for both customer and supplier. Is there a defined escalation route for problems and does any one person feel 'ownership' for the relationship? One of the most important concepts to grasp when dealing with supplier relationships is the fact that an effective relationship will not just happen. It needs to be managed, owned and developed to ensure maximum effectiveness. This ownership has to be clearly understood and defined on both sides of the relationship to ensure that maximum benefit is gained with minimum resource, and to prevent duplication of effort or missed opportunities for improvement. This module recommends the appointment of one or more Supplier Managers (see 3.1.11.1) to own the relationships with suppliers.

The review process should examine the roles and responsibilities relating to each relationship to determine whether they are still appropriate. In certain cases gaps may be found where no one owns a relationship, in others, multiple contacts may be complicating a relationship. Details of suggested roles and responsibilities can be found in Annex D.

3.1.7.5 Review existing procedures

It is important to establish what documented procedures exist, which are applicable to relationships with suppliers, which are working effectively, which are not and why not. For example, is there always an agenda for review meetings? The existence of documented procedures can provide a helpful framework for those developing the relationship. If a quality system is in operation then documented procedures will exist.

Establish whether formal change management processes are applied consistently to all existing contracts and agreements. If not, it would probably help the relationship with the supplier if such procedures were implemented.

Establish whether formal minutes with action points are issued following meetings between IT Directorate and suppliers, whether such meetings are held at an appropriate frequency, with the correct level of personnel and whether actions are carried out. If this is not the case it would be helpful to redefine how these meetings are managed.

3.1.8 Identify areas for improvement

The information gathered from the review of existing relationships and procedures will now enable proposals to be made concerning how relationships should continue and what changes and improvements are needed.

The review may determine, for example, that:

* a relationship is being managed by staff at the wrong level, perhaps with insufficient authority to make appropriate decisions, and so the people involved with this relationship will need to change

* there are so many personnel involved in dealing with a supplier that there is no continuity or satisfactory relationship able to be established

* there is no clear escalation path for issues/problems (not covered in a contract) in one or both organizations and that one needs to be agreed and established

* suppliers are having to cope with changes in customer requirements without proper notice, or customers are not given adequate notice of some planned maintenance. (Proper change control procedures in a contract or agreed documented procedures will be needed to overcome these situations and to improve relationships)

3.1.9 Initial study report and project plans

The main deliverables from the initial investigation should be:

* a report covering all the findings (the main information about existing and planned relationships should be clearly documented as it will be needed for future reference), suggestions for improvement, recommended actions and projected costs and benefits

* a project plan containing details of the next stages of the project, ie development and implementation.

3.1.9.1 The project plan

The groundwork of establishing what is important to an organization in its dealings with suppliers is now complete.

The project plan should define the tasks, deliverables, timescales, staff involvement, costs and quality control aspects for the next stages.

The plan should establish an overall timetable for the project and the stages could be as follows:

* Stage 1 - agree the objectives and deliverables for the project (3.1.10)

* Stage 2 - plan future relationships with existing and new suppliers (3.1.11 and 3.1.12)

* Stage 3 - decide the roles of customer personnel (3.1.13)

* Stage 4 - plan for security and related issues (3.1.14)

* Stage 5 - plan the continuous review of relationships and contracts (3.1.15)

* Stage 6 - implementation; start developing more effective relationships (Section 4).

An issue which should be taken into consideration during the above stages is the role of Quality Management (3.1.16).

Establishing more effective relationships is a continuous process, especially as changes of personnel take place in both customer and supplier organizations, but it is important to determine a planned end date of the project. In planning the timetable for stages 1-5, take into account the number of suppliers involved, the extent to which relationships might need to be changed and the availability of resources.

3.1.9.2   Approval

The project manager will be required to present the study report, especially the project plan, to the Project Board and management approval must be obtained to continue with the project.

3.1.10 Agree objectives and deliverables

The objectives described at 3.1.1 should be refined and amended as required following the initial study and agreed with the Project Board.

The deliverables are encompassed within some of the objectives but should include:

* a list identifying owners of relationships and those staff with management and liaison responsibilities and what their responsibilities are

* a list of all relationships classified by type and some indication of relative importance

* documented procedures covering the roles of customer personnel, review procedures, meetings etc.

3.1.11 Plan future relationships with existing suppliers

When planning future relationships with existing suppliers account must be taken of an organization's existing standards, policies and guidelines.

Ensure that all customer management and staff who are involved, are made aware that the project has moved into the planning and development stage by continuing with the awareness campaign which was begun during the initial investigation stage (see 3.1.3). The key suppliers should already be aware of the project and will hopefully have contributed to the initial investigation.

3.1.11.1 Appoint a Supplier Manager

There are many levels of communication between customer and supplier, and there is a danger of duplicated effort, opportunities being missed, or misinformation on both sides if this communication is not co-ordinated. It is important that a person within the customer organization is given responsibility to manage initial discussions with a supplier and to own this relationship in the future. This part-time role is defined as the Supplier Manager. It does not preclude liaison between other people but the Supplier Manager needs to co-ordinate interaction at other levels. The role of the Supplier Manager is discussed in section 3.3.3 and Annex D.

3.1.11.2 Initiate discussions with suppliers

The Supplier Manager should initiate discussions with each key supplier with whom there will be a continuing major relationship. Use the following guidelines when carrying out initial discussions with them.

Establish likely benefits to both parties	Establish the likely benefits to both parties of making the proposed changes in the ongoing relationship. Section 6 identifies the benefits which can be achieved with more effective relationships. Not all benefits may be achievable for all relationships. At this stage try to establish what are likely to be achievable for each individual relationship.
Assess increased costs	Assess increased costs, if any, to either party. Only if the costs can be justified should the proposed changes be carried out. Increased costs are mainly incurred in the planning and implementation stages of the project (see section 6.2).
Ascertain supplier flexibility	Ascertain whether the supplier is prepared or able to implement the proposed changes. There may be circumstances where an organization is looking for changes which the supplier is unable to implement.
	It may also be the case that a supplier is bound by company rules and practices, or changes in policy, which make it difficult to comply with a customer's wishes. For example a supplier may plan to dispense with regional Account Managers and this could affect the efficiency of existing relationships.
Analyze supplier compatibility	Analyze the compatibility of the management style and culture of the supplier with your own organization. In many cases, whilst differences should not preclude a good relationship, it becomes more difficult to reach a common understanding where significant differences exist. If this is the case consider whether these differences are a risk to the relationship and whether they can be overcome.

3.1.11.3 Agree future plans

	Once agreement on future relationships is reached in principle with the key suppliers, there are further points on more detailed, day-to-day operations to be jointly agreed.
Essential contacts	Identify essential contacts with the supplier - for example should relationships exist at senior management, administrative, end-user, or technical levels. Are there common functions in both organizations that would benefit from a relationship?
Communications	Decide how communications should be achieved. For example, who should attend review meetings? Who needs to have meetings, and who needs to have contact simply by telephone? Planned contacts and communications with suppliers should be frequent enough to meet the objectives.

For instance, where a supplier's activity is crucial to the achievement of a regular monthly customer activity, and progress monitoring is to be based upon the success of the activity, there should be a planned monthly communication. This might simply take the form of an exchange of information, but is still essential. Consider what facilities for communication are available or desirable, eg is a dial-up data link required.

Monitoring progress

Agree how progress towards the objectives can be monitored and reviewed - it is essential to establish clear success criteria and milestones towards achieving them, as well as guidelines for communicating successes to all those involved in the relationship.

Plan roles and responsibilities

Ensure that both organizations understand the essential roles required to manage the relationship:

* the Supplier Manager in a customer organization

* other managers and staff within the customer organization who have a management/liaison role

* a person in the supplier organization to own the relationship - probably a Customer Account Manager

* senior customer and supplier management to be involved in high level discussions and in the escalation of issues.

Agree dispute/ problem procedures

It is good practice to include procedures for the resolution or escalation of disputes in all agreements and plans. Issues should be addressed jointly by both organizations. In particular it is beneficial to establish a clear procedure for handling sensitive issues such as poor performance by personnel on either side.

It is likely that the agreed procedures resulting from a discussion of the above points will entail much more proactive communication between the two organizations as well as the establishment of some more formal channels.

3.1.12 Plan relationships with new suppliers

It is important to establish effective relationships with new suppliers as early as possible. Take into account the relevant guidelines stated at section 3.1.11.2, and the lessons learned from reviewing existing relationships. In discussions with prospective new suppliers and when defining Statement of Service Requirements, consider what relationship issues should be included such as contact points, methods of communication, reporting etc. New relationships must be properly planned, developed and managed by the customer in line with agreed improved existing practices.

3.1.13 Decide the roles of customer personnel

3.1.13.1 Within IT Services

A brief summary of how the IT Infrastructure Library views the roles and responsibilities of customer personnel, and in particular the managers of IT Service functions, in relation to suppliers is given at Annex D. This provides a starting point for defining which personnel should be involved in the review of the nature and operation of existing supplier relationships.

Some or all of these roles may currently exist in a customer organization and some important ones may not be allocated. It is important to plan how these roles are fulfilled, taking account of the skills available and the current and future relationships which will exist with suppliers. Depending on the size and structure of an organization, in particular the IT Directorate, and the types of supplier relationships which exist:

* multiple roles may be fulfilled by the same person

* one role, spanning several relationships may be given to a person

* some roles and responsibilities may not be appropriate or will be merged.

If as a result of reviewing relationships with suppliers, it is planned to change the roles of individual personnel in those relationships, then this must be notified to the suppliers involved explaining briefly the reasons and the changes to be made. The increase in the importance of effective communications may change the emphasis, if not the roles, of IT managers and staff.

Decide whether, as a result of planned changes, any training is required for managers and staff and plan accordingly. Qualities and skills required are discussed in more detail at section 3.3.5 and Annex H and training requirements at section 3.3.6.

3.1.13.2 Business manager involvement

Where customer organizations are moving to a greater involvement by business managers in managing IT resources, then it is likely to be more appropriate for a business manager, rather than a manager from IT Services, to "own" a relationship with a supplier and act as the Supplier Manager.

Business areas will increasingly become budget holders for the provision of IT services and they will want:

* increased involvement in how their services are provided

* greater influence on the selection of suppliers of services.

Where long term, more strategic, relationships are planned, these will normally involve the exchange of business information as well as information on IT practices and policy. Business managers need to be involved in these relationships.

Where an organization contracts out its IT service provision, business managers will become the intelligent customer and will have functional responsibility for managing the relationship (see section 3.0.3.3).

Business managers are the recipients of the IT services to which suppliers are contributing or providing, and should have been made aware of the review of supplier relationships at an early stage (see section 3.1.3). In a contracted-out situation they would be responsible for the review.

3.1.14 Plan for security and related issues

Customer organizations are likely to have a security policy which covers access to premises, facilities and information, by third parties. Such policies within government departments should be part of the management and technical policies defined in the IS strategy and be compliant with government IT Security Policy.

In contractual relationships security issues should be clearly identified and understood by both parties. They may include:

* the role of an IT Security Officer within government departments (see Annex D.8)

* the security of remote links and the use of remote diagnostics

* the ownership of customer and related data and software held at suppliers' data centres

* the requirements relating to the avoidance of malicious software

* monitoring and reviewing of security arrangements.

For an organization which has contracted out its IT service provision the responsibility for security must remain with the organization, although some of the functions can be contracted out to the external supplier.

Security issues should also be borne in mind in any non-contractual relationship, eg:

* the protection of, and access to, data and information by both customer and suppliers

* the physical security of a customer installation

* the need to maintain an awareness of security policies and practices by all relevant staff.

The customer should also be aware of its responsibilities to ensure confidentiality of its information, eg under the terms of the Data Protection Act 1984, Computer Misuse Act 1990.

Non-disclosure

Suppliers have commercially sensitive information, usually relating to their planned products and activities, which they may be reluctant to disclose to a customer. However, where suppliers have a strategic relationship with a customer and they believe that knowledge of a planned product or service may be useful to that customer, then they are often willing to supply information under a special agreement. Similarly a customer who is formulating a new strategy as a result of a political initiative, and is working closely with a supplier, may want that supplier to sign an agreement.

A non-disclosure agreement is simply an agreement not to disclose to a third party information given which is subject to the agreement. It is important to establish procedures to minimize the risk, or increase the chances of detection, of confidentiality rules being breached and to clearly allocate responsibility for maintaining non-disclosure agreements on both sides.

Guidance on IT security matters is available to central government departments in the CCTA **IT Security Library**.

3.1.15 Plan future reviews of relationships and contracts

3.1.15.1 Review of relationships

When a long-term relationship is about to be established it is important to plan to conduct regular reviews of that relationship after say the first six months and then annually. Decide who to involve, how to measure the effectiveness and progress achieved and how to identify follow-up actions (see 5.1.4 and 5.1.5).

3.1.15.2 Review and maintenance of contracts

Situations and circumstances change, and there may be a need to change the contract to reflect this. Suggested procedures for maintaining the integrity of the contract are listed in Annex G.

There is a need to plan for regular contract reviews using formal change management procedures when necessary. Whilst reviews of, and amendments to, contracts are the responsibility of the Purchasing and Contracts Section, they are of relevance to relationships and the Supplier Manager needs to be aware of any changes.

3.1.16 Consider the role of quality management

An important influence on the quality of service provided by an IT service provider is the quality of the products, services and procedures of their external suppliers. The IT service provider must ensure that these aspects of service provision are of the desired quality and contracts with suppliers should specify agreed quality goals against which their performance will be measured.

Many large IT suppliers either already have, or are in the process of obtaining, certification to the BS 5750/ISO 9000 series of quality management standards for the development and delivery of products and services. Organizations may wish to check with existing suppliers, for whom quality certification was not a criteria at the time of selection, whether they have achieved or are applying for certification, and if so whether it is for:

* the part of the supplier organization with which they are dealing

* the service(s) to be purchased

* the process by which equipment to be purchased is produced.

Whilst certification does not guarantee the quality of service provision it indicates a willingness and capability on the part of a supplier to monitor and seek to improve it.

An organization may wish to make the achievement of quality certification a prerequisite to entering into any long-term relationship with an IT supplier. However it is worth remembering that this may eliminate smaller suppliers who cannot afford certification, and must not be used to unfairly reduce competition. Guidance on planning and implementing a quality management system for IT service management is provided in the IT Infrastructure Library module **Quality Management for IT Services** and in the CCTA **Quality Management Library**.

3.2 Dependencies

Planning to improve and develop customer and supplier relationships is dependent on several factors which are discussed at sections 3.2.1 to 3.2.4 below. One general dependency is the commitment of individual staff. Every individual has to be responsible for the success of their element of managing supplier relationships. All customer personnel should be encouraged to look for ways of improving the relationship with their contacts in the supplier organization and this may require them to undergo training (see 3.3.6).

3.2.1 Management commitment

The most important prerequisite is the active support and commitment of senior management, particularly the IT Director, but also senior business management. They must be convinced that there are worthwhile benefits to be gained from establishing more effective relationships and that any changes will be in line with the organization's objectives.

Senior management may already have established relationships with their counterparts in major suppliers. It is important that these relationships are included in the review of the existing situation. They need to take a committed active part in the awareness campaign and to "practice what they preach" in dealing with their own contacts in supplier organizations.

3.2.2 Associated functions

Associated functions need to be in place and working effectively before embarking upon discussions with suppliers, such as:

* well defined purchasing procedures

* effective change control procedures

* effective communication channels.

3.2.3 Changes in working practices

Changes may be needed at the operational, as well as the management level, to reallocate responsibilities for liaison with suppliers, or to implement new procedures such as the introduction of formal minuting of all meetings. Plan how these changes will be agreed and implemented and ensure that there is effective management of change.

3.2.4 Existing Projects

Where the establishment of effective supplier relationships is being undertaken as part of an existing project, the success of the initiative may be dependent on activities in the overall project. For example if it is established as an adjunct to a Quality Management System (QMS) it is essential for the plans and procedures to reflect the principles of the QMS.

3.3 People

Relationship issues permeate an entire organization and are not peculiar to IT Services or to the IT Directorate as a whole. All management and staff who have contact with suppliers have a responsibility for ensuring that relationships work effectively. The module draws the distinction between:

* the ownership of a relationship by a Supplier Manager who has overall responsibility for that relationship (see section 3.1.11.1)

* management roles, where by definition the persons have some authority in controlling the relationship

* liaison roles which are concerned more with communicating and maintaining contact with suppliers.

The distinction between management and liaison roles is brought out in a description at Annex D of the more important of these roles and responsibilities within a customer organization.

As a result of reviewing relationships more or fewer staff may have contacts with suppliers and the nature of existing contacts may change. If clear channels of communication are available the supplier contact becomes more focused and meaningful, leading to a more constructive, quality relationship.

3.3.1 Internal business customers

The term internal business customer is used in this module to describe a business area consisting of both business managers who specify requirements for IT services and end-users (who may include business managers) who use IT services. Business managers are responsible for communicating the business need for IT support to either the IT Directorate, when service provision is in-house, or the external supplier via the intelligent customer function, when service provision is contracted out. Business managers and end-users can also provide valuable feedback on service quality.

3.3.2 IT Services

Where service provision remains in-house, IT Services has overall responsibility for the operational IT services provided to its customers. It ensures that the IT service requirements of its customers are provided as cost effectively as possible based on negotiated Service Level Agreements. IT Services is likely to have most involvement with suppliers and its need to establish effective relationships is therefore of paramount importance.

3.3.3 Supplier Manager

It is essential that the responsibility for owning the relationship between a customer and suppliers is clearly established in the role of the Supplier Manager (see 3.1.11.1).

Depending on the amount of contact required, it may be appropriate to have one or a combination of the following:

* in the case of a number of suppliers with limited involvement with a customer - a person acting as Supplier Manager for all the suppliers

* in the case of a major supplier to a customer - a person acting as Supplier Manager for the one supplier.

This role of Supplier Manager is likely to involve formalizing an existing, but informal, liaison role which someone in the customer organization already fulfils, such as the manager of an IT Services function (for example the Service Level Manager), or a business manager. The consequences of not formalizing this role could be misdirected information, confusion and much wasted time on both sides.

The Supplier Manager mirrors the role of Account Manager in a supplier organization and should be the prime contact for both supplier and customer personnel on issues concerning a particular relationship. The Supplier Manager should be kept aware of communications between his/her supplier(s) and other customer personnel and also acts as a facilitator in arranging official meetings, informal discussions and joint social activities. The Supplier Manager should become familiar with the supplier organization and know who to liaise with on a wide range of issues.

The role is unlikely to be full time; it could be allocated to one of several managers of IT Services functions such as the Service Level Manager or the Availability Manager, or if appropriate a business manager. Annex D gives more details on the role and responsibilities of a Supplier Manager.

3.3.4 Suppliers

Currently there is much greater motivation within supplier organizations to have a person who is an Account Manager, responsible for the success of the supplier's relationship with a customer and for dealing with any issues which may arise. In many cases the Account Manager is empowered within the supplier organization to make decisions on a variety of topics ranging from discounts through to resource issues.

Though the Account Manager is empowered to make decisions, it may not be the most senior relationship between the organization and the supplier. Responsibility is delegated to the Account Manager to bring decision-making closer to the customer and improve the quality of service offered.

In many cases there will be senior level contact where a supplier has a strategic relationship with an organization. This is likely to involve an exchange of senior management views on a variety of topics of relevance to the relationship.

3.3.5 Qualities and skills

Certain qualities and skills are desirable in the personnel involved in managing supplier relationships and these are set out in Annex H. The greater the involvement of the person the more importance the qualities and skills assume and this is particularly true for the Supplier Manager.

If people without the right qualities and skills are selected then the potential for actually worsening the relationships rather than improving them is significantly increased.

3.3.6 Training

During the planning stage, make an assessment of any training needs of personnel who are to be involved with suppliers. It may be necessary for those involved directly in managing supplier relationships to have particular training in the skills and qualities referred to at Annex H, for example effective communication and assertiveness. Consider mounting general awareness training of supplier relationships in the form of seminars, in order to reach as wide an audience as possible.

In some cases where it is essential to get a good understanding of both customer and supplier organizations, it may be beneficial for a customer employee to have a short period of secondment in the supplier organization. Some suppliers will happily reciprocate in this arrangement.

Training should be concerned with the needs and benefits of better supplier relationships and the ways in which behaviour changes may facilitate this.

It might be more productive to view the training required as part of professional development training, ie training in interpersonal skills, or negotiating skills and not limit its scope to the supplier relationship context.

3.4 Timing

When planning to improve the management of supplier relationships there is rarely a convenient time to start planning changes. However, this should not be taken as a reason to do nothing.

Plan to either introduce the improvement programme gradually taking one supplier at a time, or it may be more appropriate in a small customer organization to plan a combined programme for all suppliers running in parallel.

3.4.1 Part of a quality initiative

Where it is planned to incorporate a supplier relationships project as part of an existing quality management initiative (see 3.1), then the timing may well be defined by the quality project.

3.4.2 Priorities

The priority of each relationship should already have been agreed earlier (see section 3.1.5). However, there are events and priorities which may make it important to improve relationships with suppliers more quickly than would otherwise happen. These could be that:

* a major new contract is to be let, for example, as a result of market testing

* an existing contract with a supplier is in dispute and causing serious problems

* there have been serious personality clashes in relationships with supplier's representatives.

Events of this nature may not allow for a well planned approach to be taken. They may require that effort is concentrated on one supplier, which may or may not fit in with the overall priorities for supplier relationships which have been established.

It is necessary to balance short-term, and possibly urgent needs, with longer term objectives. It is also important to plan for sufficient resources to implement any changes. Since there are usually less resources than one would wish, the setting of priorities becomes more important.

4. Implementation

4.1 Procedures

This section describes the implementation stage of the project. This is a combination of initial activities (see 4.1.1) and beginning to establish more effective relationships by:

* developing relationships (4.1.2)

* developing effective communications (4.1.3)

* carrying out the agreed training programme (4.1.4)

* encouraging feedback (4.1.5)

* attending relevant events (4.1.6)

* dealing with disputes and disagreements (4.1.7)

* properly delegating responsibility (4.1.8)

* dealing with complex relationships (4.1.9)

* managing changes (4.1.10).

4.1.1 Initial activities

Assignment of personnel

The Supplier Manager(s) should have been appointed during the planning stage (see 3.1.11.1). Other customer personnel, in particular the managers of IT Services functions involved in implementing effective supplier relationships (see section 3.1.13), should now take on their assigned roles. Make any new appointments which were identified as being required and commence any necessary training.

Awareness campaign

Continue with the awareness campaign (see 3.1.3 and 3.1.11) to internal and supplier personnel. This should now cover:

* the planned implementation

* the roles and responsibilities of individuals and the interfaces being established

* the benefits to be gained.

It is important to retain the commitment of suppliers to the relationships.

Establish communication channels

Establish the organizational channels needed to achieve effective internal and external communications as defined in section 3.1.11. This will involve matching the roles within the customer organization to their opposite number in the supplier's organization and ensuring that all planned communication links, eg facsimile, data links, are in place.

Meeting structures and reports	Establish and agree the meeting structures and report formats required to support the relationships. These should be kept as simple as possible.
Change control	Ensure that change control procedures within the customer organization are understood and agreed by all concerned.
Arrange initial meetings	The Supplier Manager should arrange initial meetings with each supplier concerned as agreed during the planning stage (see 3.1.11.2). At these meetings:

* confirm the involvement of customer and supplier personnel in the on-going relationship

* ensure that opposite numbers meet and understand each other's roles

* identify any existing problems and determine the appropriate course of action required

* set dates for future review meetings - experience suggests that formal contract or relationship reviews tend to be held more frequently for new or problematic relationships (possibly monthly), and less frequently for well established satisfactory ones (possibly every six months).

It may also be appropriate to:

* invite the supplier to give a short presentation about their company and operations and allow time for questions

* plan to visit one another's sites as this often helps get a good understanding of essential procedures and provides an opportunity to meet appropriate personnel.

4.1.2 Develop supplier relationships

4.1.2.1 Understand responsibilities and actions

For relationships to be successful there must be a clear understanding by both parties of the responsibilities and expectations of the other in particular contractual situations. However, for long-term relationships a spirit of mutual interest and co-operation needs to be achieved and maintained beyond the contract. This can be brought about by regular and open discussions held within the framework of communications which were planned for the relationship.

Where successful and productive relationships are being developed it is important to give credit and recognize improvements. However, difficult situations involving negative feedback on supplier performance will arise, and these should be dealt with in an unemotional, objective and constructive way.

4.1.2.2 Personal relationships

Friendly but professional (efficient, honest and courteous) relationships are needed between customer and suppliers and most suppliers are as anxious as their customers to deal with any problems such as clashes of personality. Perhaps the most difficult of such situations is that in which one of the supplier's staff proves unacceptable to the customer. Similarly the customer should be prepared to listen and take action when the supplier raises questions of customer competency or behaviour. Procedures for dealing with problems of this type should already have been agreed during the planning phase (see section 3.1.11.3)

4.1.2.3 On-site administrator

Where a long-term strategic relationship is beginning or already exists, there may be a case for a person from the supplier organization to take on a role of an on-site administrator who effectively becomes part of the customer team whilst working via a network link with the supplier's own systems. Suppliers heavily involved with a customer are often willing to provide this service, since an on-site administrator can cover many topics, such as training, order taking, delivery progressing etc. The presence of an on-site administrator facilitates closer personnel liaison between the supplier and the customer's Supplier Manager.

4.1.3 Develop effective communications

The type and method of communications agreed during the planning phase (see section 3.1.10.3) should now be implemented. Establish contacts and start the regular review meetings between the agreed customer and supplier personnel. Use the procedures agreed for the resolution and escalation of disputes (see 4.1.7 for more detail). However it is important to communicate satisfaction as well as complaints and to do this whilst knowledge of events is current.

Effective communication implies listening and understanding as well as giving information. Most suppliers want a customer to be proactive in advising or informing them of changes and problems which may affect the work in hand.

Ad-hoc meetings and reports

Even in the most well regulated relationship there is always the need for ad-hoc reports and meetings to deal with unexpected situations. These situations may take the form of either a crisis or a major change which was not foreseen. In these circumstances circulate reports to an agreed list of people and include all interested parties in meetings.

Agree the participants with the supplier to ensure attendance of the correct level of people on both sides. This is essential if decisions are to be made quickly in any crisis.

4.1.4 Training

Any training requirement identified as an area for improvement (see section 3.3.6) should now be put into effect. Ideally complete the training of personnel directly involved in the program before the start-up meetings. Training events can range from attendance at formal courses to seminars, workshops and counselling by line managers or others. One-off or standard courses or events may be recommended. It may be appropriate to invite major suppliers to participate in some events.

4.1.5 Encourage feedback

Particularly during the early stages of implementing more effective relationships, it is important to encourage feedback. The objective of giving feedback is always to seek an improvement in a situation.

Set general rules for feedback. Always make it:

* constructive and objective

    - when reporting problems or difficulties, if possible or appropriate, try to suggest solutions, or at least try to give an indication of the approach to be taken in defining the solution

    - try to avoid adding emotion or making accusations; this is always counter productive

- report on both successful and unsatisfactory
events or work

* detailed and accurate

- whether providing feedback on problems or
successes try to give an example and evidence

- if it is known that malpractice has contributed to
a problem or disagreement do not hide this; it
will only complicate the solution

* timely - delays can mean that it loses impact or is too
late to act upon

* mutual - always be prepared to listen to as well as
give feedback.

There may be a formal problem management function
within an organization for dealing with IT service problems
but it may be appropriate to have defined procedures for
dealing with other formal feedback concerning
relationships. However informal feedback should also be
encouraged to help generate an open and honest
relationship.

Ensure that feedback is communicated to the correct person
or level in the organization who can initiate remedial
action. When feedback is received, always report to the
initiator the actions that will be taken, or if appropriate, that
action will not be taken.

4.1.6 Attending relevant events

Customers and suppliers can often gain considerable
benefit from being involved in events such as user group
meetings or presentations held by customers. These provide
an opportunity to meet personnel from each organization,
often informally, and can provide a useful forum to develop
a better understanding and to generally discuss issues.
These events however should not be used to replace the
agreed regular review meetings (see 4.1.2).

4.1.6.1 User Group meetings

Most major suppliers have independently organized User
Groups associated with major products or services, and
there are also independent special interest groups. These
groups usually hold regular meetings which, whilst still a
forum for the exchange of technical ideas, also cover many
issues of interest. They provide an opportunity for a general
exchange of information, ideas and problems between
suppliers and customers.

4.1.6.2 Customer presentations and conferences

When a relevant presentation is given by a customer to internal staff it may be appropriate to invite major suppliers to attend. This can provide an opportunity for suppliers to learn more of the customer's future business direction and may enable them to contribute ideas to help the customer in achieving future business objectives and improving service. Useful contacts can often be made.

There are also often conferences of people and organizations engaged in similar areas of work. It may be mutually beneficial to invite a supplier representative.

4.1.7 Disputes and disagreements

When disputes arise with a supplier it is seldom a viable option to solve them by terminating the contract. Contractual relationships should have clear escalation paths and well documented procedures for dealing with all types of dispute.

It is essential for both parties to feel the need to resolve the issue. Anything which threatens the relationship is a problem for both parties not just either supplier or customer. The question to be asked is "how do WE solve the issue?"

4.1.7.1 Speedy resolution

The faster that issues can be resolved, the less damage is done to the relationship. There is less likelihood of the issues becoming serious disputes between the two parties and there is less time for people to adopt rigid or emotional positions.

4.1.7.2 Ownership of problems

Clear delineation of responsibilities will reduce the number of disputes, but where it is not clear, perhaps the least productive way of seeking a resolution to a dispute is to deny any responsibility for it and blame the other party.

Resolve problems jointly with suppliers where possible. Allocating blame and stating contractual liabilities is not the most efficient or economic way of solving the problem.

Undertake resolution of issues in a spirit of co-operation not confrontation.

4.1.7.3   Escalation

Deal with issues at the lowest level possible within an organization. Unnecessary involvement of senior management causes bad feeling on both sides and wastes valuable time. It is essential that escalation procedures are well understood by all concerned to ensure fast, effective resolution to any issues.

4.1.8   Delegation

Both supplier and customer personnel who have agreed to take responsibility for any aspect of a relationship, should not delegate this without good reason. It is important that they remain committed to their roles or use a formal review process to make any changes. If delegation takes place then the person must be fully briefed and should always report back results to the person who gave them the task.

4.1.9   Complex relationships

Where a contract, or contracts, for a complex piece of work are in place, there may be several suppliers to deal with or the relationship may be with a prime contractor.

Where there is a prime contractor, it is essential that all interactions with sub-contractors are regulated by the prime contractor. If required build communications interfaces with sub-contractors into the procedures agreed with the prime contractor. Where it might be advantageous to hold discussions directly with a sub-contractor, only do this with the knowledge and participation of the prime contractor.

4.1.10 Managing changes

4.1.10.1 Managing changing roles

The supplier management and liaison roles initially agreed within the customer organization will probably change over time. Some will be found to be unnecessary, others will grow in importance. Address these changes at internal reviews to ensure that the actual roles at any time, are still manageable by the incumbent and are still meeting a real need for the organization.

4.1.10.2 Organizational and developmental changes

From time to time there are staff changes and perhaps more major changes in the way that an organization is structured, or in its work and objectives. These events may have an effect on the functioning of supplier management and perhaps suppliers.

Succession planning

Cater for any change of personnel by succession planning. Some organizations have a formal method of doing this. Where this is so, follow the method for supplier management, as for other functions. Where there is no defined way of doing this every person who is involved in supplier management could be asked to nominate possible successors.

Communicate changes

It is essential at times of major change that senior customer management communicate these changes to the senior management of the suppliers. Credibility will be lost where news is badly communicated, via an unofficial source. Similar actions should of course be taken by suppliers when there are major changes within their organization, or one of their key staff is moving.

4.2 Dependencies

The most important dependency is the active support and commitment of senior management. Their commitment to the process of change must be demonstrated through making themselves accessible to suppliers when the need arises.

The training identified during the planning stage (see section 3.1.13.1) must be carried out wherever possible prior to personnel taking on their new responsibilities.

Fulfil other dependencies described in section 3.2 prior to implementing new procedures.

4.3 People

Once roles and responsibilities have been agreed, any necessary organizational and personnel changes must be implemented. Often these changes may only be formalizing and regulating what already exists rather than the creation of new posts or responsibilities.

4.4 Timing

Once the initial activities, referred to at 4.1.1, have taken place, developing more effective relationships can begin. The time taken to implement the new approach will depend on:

* the number of suppliers to an organization

* the way an organization functions

* the culture of the organization.

Where the culture of an organization is consultative and open to new ideas, then it is likely that the project will take less time to implement than in an organization which has a fixed hierarchy and is directive by nature.

5.   Post-implementation and audit

5.1   Procedures

5.1.1   Introduction

If the establishment of effective relationships has been managed as a project a formal Project Evaluation Review should be carried out. When sufficient time has elapsed to assess the success (or otherwise) of the project, as measured against the declared objectives, a Post-Implementation Review (PIR) should take place. Whether there was a formal project or not, there is a need for continuous monitoring of the effectiveness of relationships, either undertaken on the basis of reviews of individual supplier relationships by the Supplier Manager or as general reviews to monitor the overall effectiveness of supplier relationships.

Where a quality management system is in operation in an organization, auditing of documented procedures concerning supplier relationships will need to be carried out by internal or external auditors.

5.1.2   Project Evaluation Review

At the end of a formal project the Project Manager should review how effectively the project was carried out and produce a Project Evaluation Report for the Project Board which identifies:

*   achievement against planned targets, critical success factors and objectives

*   conformance to project timescales and estimated costs

*   the general success of the project

*   how project personnel performed their roles

*   lessons to be learnt

*   problems encountered and how they were resolved

*   any ongoing issues which need to be progressed and monitored.

5.1.3   Post-Implementation Review

Where a formal project approach was used a PIR should be held within an agreed period after the end of the project, say after six to nine months. The PIR should examine

whether more effective supplier relationships have been
achieved and whether stated objectives are being met. The
review should be convened by the IT Services Manager and
include:

* Supplier Managers

* other managers of IT Service functions who have
  significant contact with suppliers

* business managers as appropriate

* supplier representatives.

The review should determine whether for example:

* both customer and supplier personnel feel that
  improvements in relationships have been achieved

* the agreed roles and responsibilities of customer
  personnel involved in relationships are appropriate

* cost benefits have been achieved

* initial performance measures are satisfactory.

The output of the PIR should be a set of jointly agreed
actions aimed at achieving further improvements. The
review should also agree the cycle for subsequent reviews
of supplier relationships (see 5.1.5).

5.1.4 Monitoring effectiveness

Continuous monitoring and evaluation of the process of
supplier relationships is important because relationships
need to be continually reassessed and cultivated, especially
if there are changes in personnel involved in the
relationships.

Monitoring can be implemented in a number of ways, for
example:

* including supplier relationships on the agenda at
  internal IT management meetings ensures that the
  topic is regularly discussed and gives an opportunity
  for issues to be raised

* obtaining feedback from suppliers at review
  meetings (see 4.1.3)

* carrying out customer surveys of IT Services
  managers and business managers to obtain their
  views.

The Supplier Manager should collate and analyze the feedback from all the relevant parties and this will provide input to the formal review process (see 5.1.5). If required, as part of monitoring, particular programmes can be put in place to monitor specific areas of concern.

It is often difficult to identify criteria which can be used to measure the effectiveness of relationships and inevitably there is an element of subjective judgement on the part of individuals. However examples of related measures which could be used are:

* the level of communication from both the customer organization and suppliers via the Supplier Manager and the on-going trend

* the number of problems identified, eg when the supplier does not deliver as specified in a contract and the customer business suffers

* the number of invocations of escalation procedures

* the number of invoices being submitted by a supplier either late, requiring amendment or requiring resubmission

* the number of meetings held between customer and suppliers (co-ordination by the Supplier Manager should lead to a reduction)

* the responsiveness of customer and suppliers to issues raised.

5.1.5 Reviewing for efficiency and effectiveness

At periodic intervals, usually annually, the IT Services Manager should carry out a more formal review of customer and supplier relationships. Review procedures for their efficiency and effectiveness in achieving the objectives which were set (see 3.1.1). A flowchart of the process is shown in Figure 6, overleaf.

Initially establish a review timetable. During the formal review, assess:

* the overall effectiveness of relationships between customer and suppliers

* whether individual personnel involved in supplier relationships are performing effectively

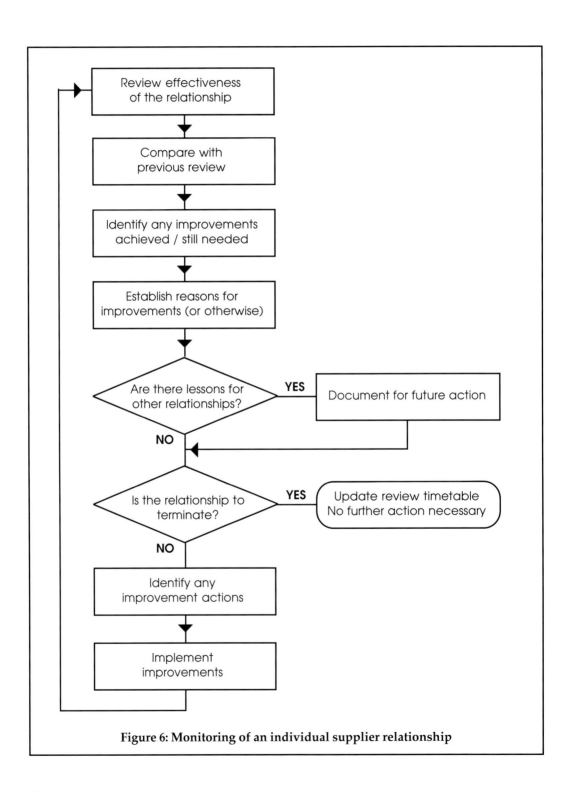

Figure 6: Monitoring of an individual supplier relationship

* the effectiveness with which defined management and liaison roles (see Annex D) are being fulfilled

* the effectiveness of communications with suppliers

* the effectiveness of the resolution of disputes or disagreements

* senior customer and supplier management commitment

* the level of co-operation from IT service managers and business managers with the Supplier Manager(s)

* the benefits of the improved practices and procedures

* the costs of maintaining relationships.

The review should identify any trends in relationships, and whether any procedures have fallen into disuse. Where procedures have proved unacceptable to either customer or supplier, this issue should have been raised as part of ongoing feedback from either party. If so, check that the required changes to overcome the problem have been implemented, and if not, why not.

For any organization with a Quality Management System, the nature and content of the review of supplier management procedures should comply with the quality system requirements. For further guidance on quality system management see the **Quality Management for IT Services** module of the IT Infrastructure Library and the CCTA **Quality Management Library**.

It may help to re-apply the checklist of questions used at the start of the project for assessing the situation at that time (see Annex C). The answers to these questions will give a qualitative indication of improvements.

External factors

In addition to reviewing internal operations the review should take account of external factors which can influence the success or otherwise of supplier relationships. For example changes in the following could impact on supplier relationships:

* a private sector company being the subject of a takeover bid or merger

* government policy - a government department may change to Agency status which may affect how it contracts for its IT services in future

* direction of a supplier's business - they may be moving from being a services supplier into the Systems Integration business

* new technology - the availability of a new range of products from a supplier

* economic climate - in a recession suppliers are keener to keep and win business which could either lead to greater emphasis on improving customer service or a reluctance to commit resources to the relationship activity.

Contract compliance

It is useful to hold contract reviews with suppliers either six monthly or annually. Reviews should be undertaken by the Purchasing and Contracts Section and might usefully follow or be combined with a general review meeting with suppliers.

Many customers and suppliers regard contracts, once agreed and signed, to be of secondary importance where there is a good relationship, and a last recourse when there is a bad one. However, the contract should clearly define what is to be supplied, when, how and at what price. It should also be kept up to date via the change control procedure defined at the beginning of the project.

Deviations from contract compliance, by either customer or supplier, need to be investigated and remedied either by an agreed change to contractual terms, or by actions to facilitate and ensure full compliance. Annex G describes various methods for updating contracts.

5.1.6 Management reporting

The report from the Post-Implementation Review and subsequent efficiency and effectiveness reviews should be distributed to appropriate IT senior management and senior business managers.

Whilst the review cycle will provide a snapshot of the status of relationships, the framework put in place to support supplier relationships should provide a continuous record of events.

The procedures for change control and the resolution of disputes should each have produced a documentary record of how events have been dealt with. Copies of minutes of meetings held with suppliers should be retained by the appointed Supplier Manager and should be available to senior management if requested.

5.1.7 Auditing for compliance/ conformance

Where a customer organization operates a Quality Management System (QMS), quality audits should be carried out. Audit is a mandatory element of any QMS which conforms to the quality management standard BS 5750/ISO 9000 series. Relationships with suppliers should be covered by internal quality procedures.

Security audits will also be required. These will cover compliance testing of agreed protective measures and review of the effectiveness of security procedures (see 3.1.14).

A QMS is an internal management tool for the examination and review of business functions and it is recommended that an audit is carried out at least annually. In the context of supplier relationships the following general points should be taken into consideration during any audit:

* have terms of reference and objectives for each supplier relationship been drawn up?

* has responsibility for relationships with each supplier been clearly allocated to a single Supplier Manager?

* have any agreed administrative procedures been properly documented and used?

* has a timetable of joint review meetings been established with all key suppliers?

The QMS audit is sponsored by the organization's IT Director and either internal auditors from within the customer organization, who are from outside the area to be audited, or independent external auditors, may be used.

The auditors should produce a report for IT senior management for review with Supplier Managers. Agree any remedial action between all parties, document it and ensure that it is carried out.

For guidance on a general approach to auditing all infrastructure management activities refer to the IT Infrastructure Library **Quality Management for IT Services** module and the CCTA **Quality Management Library**.

5.2   Dependencies

The major dependency on senior management commitment and support will remain. The continued success of supplier relationships is also dependent on changes in management or changes in the structure of an organization not being allowed to jeopardize the continuation of good relationships.

5.3   People

The people who contribute to the review process should be those who are involved in supplier relationships (see 3.1.13). The Post-Implementation Review is initiated by the person who was the Project Manager but should be carried out by someone not directly involved in the project. Future reviews should be initiated by the Supplier Manager's line management.

The Supplier Manager(s) will be involved in the reviews and it may also be the case that personnel who manage other functions within the customer organization can make a contribution to the review process and the actions which arise from it.

Where an audit has been notified or requested the Supplier Manager should provide the auditor with a list of relevant personnel and their defined roles to facilitate carrying out the audit.

5.4   Timing

Carry out the Post-Implementation Review between 6-9 months after the end of the project, allowing sufficient time for changes to take effect.

An appropriate review cycle should be set for efficiency and effectiveness reviews. The time periods involved will depend on the extent of changes required but would not usually be less than six months nor greater than annual.

6. Benefits, costs and possible problems

6.1 Benefits

6.1.1 General benefits

Establishing effective customer and supplier relationships and understanding the issues involved provides many benefits. Some will be intangible and can only be identified by a general feeling of satisfaction within the organization, expressed by the people involved in the relationships. Examples of intangible benefits are that there will be:

* a level of trust between customer and supplier

* an understanding by each organization of the issues, difficulties, capabilities and requirements of the other

* a professional approach to managing relationships

* well publicized and established personal contacts

* better investment decisions made due to being better informed

* lower risk involved when there is a high dependency on key suppliers.

More measurable benefits should result from there being:

* fewer major problems to address

* less unproductive time spent finding the right contacts once there is a defined ownership of relationships

* less time spent on negotiating contracts

* properly focused and informed meetings between customer and supplier

* a lower level of spend on contingency

* a reduction in the impact and cost of changes, which are imposed by suppliers, due to earlier notification and discussion

* an improvement in meeting target dates by suppliers.

The customer will, for example, feel more confident that the supplier will meet target dates when these are agreed, thus not feel the need to set artificially tight targets to allow for slippage. On the other hand, suppliers will be more inclined to do all they can to meet a tight deadline if they know that it is genuine.

6.1.2 Benefits to internal business customers

The internal business customers of the IT services being provided will see specific benefits. These include:

* a more efficient resolution of supplier-related problems as a result of the supplier having a better understanding of the business priorities of the problems raised

* improved reliability and availability of the service from the IT Directorate, which stems directly from the better relationship between the IT Directorate and its suppliers.

6.1.3 Benefits to the IT Directorate

The IT Directorate will benefit from:

* potential problems being raised and resolved quickly, with fewer becoming major issues needing senior management involvement

* IT Service Managers having increased information and understanding of the supplier organization, clear lines of communication with the key personnel and hence confidence in the supplier's ability to deliver to the required quality and on time, for a given cost

* in long-term relationships, improved dialogue between the Directorate and suppliers resulting in better long-term awareness of developments, new products etc, leading to better planning and management of IT service provision.

6.1.4 Benefits to the supplier

The supplier also benefits from being able to:

* forecast resource requirements more accurately because of an increased knowledge of customer requirements

* prioritize resources better

* decrease the cost of sales to a customer because of a better understanding of the way the customer organization works and what its requirements are

* forecast its revenues more accurately.

6.2 Costs

Organizations should regard money and time spent on the improvement of customer and supplier relationships as an investment for the future. However the costs have to be weighed against the benefits and justified. The potential payback in terms of realizing better value for money as discussed in section 6.1, should more than justify the expense.

The initial costs of improving relationships will occur in the planning and implementation stages and will be mainly in the areas of:

* training of customer personnel

* working on new procedures to improve internal communications or streamline invoice payment etc

* possible reallocation of responsibilities within a customer's IT Directorate

* possible use of consultancy services.

On-going costs of managing relationships more effectively will be higher in a long-term relationship. However it may be possible to reduce some costs if there is currently duplication of effort, eg by reducing the number of customer managers needing to attend meetings with suppliers, and by better co-ordination of activities.

6.3 Possible problems

There are a number of possible problems which may arise in establishing more effective customer and supplier relationships. These include:

* senior management commitment is missing in one or other of the organizations

* the customer has no suitable Supplier Managers

* the potential conflict between developing a close working relationship with a supplier and the need to use competitive tendering to ensure best value for money (Suppliers should accept that customers will wish to keep competitive tendering as an option for future purchases)

* people stopping working at a relationship once it has been improved, leading to a decline or stagnation in that relationship

* the potential difficulty in changing some relationships, which have been in existence for a considerable time, but which have been ineffective

* a lack of clarification of roles and responsibilities

* the difficulty of maintaining good relationships at all levels and avoiding either party trying to 'go over people's heads' straight to senior management

* new work practices and procedures not being followed by one or other of the organizations

* the potential difficulty in understanding the other organization's goals and objectives

* the initial cost of implementation

* the difficulty of finishing some relationships.

For public sector organizations, government policy and EC legislation may be a factor in determining what types of relationships organizations are allowed to enter into, but this does not prohibit the improvement of existing customer and supplier relationships.

7.   Tools

Managing relationships is an activity requiring good inter-personal skills, ie it is a people-oriented activity which cannot be automated. However, support for underpinning tasks can be provided by the basic office automation facilities such as word processing, electronic mail, spreadsheet and database tools. In addition account planning and workflow analysis methodologies can be used to ensure a joint understanding and good communication.

There are suppliers' management systems which can be used for contract management to, for example, calculate maintenance credits, monitor support levels and operational performance in a contractual situation. There are also proprietary products used to control the tendering process, for example to assist in drawing up service specifications, producing contracts, and to manage customer and contractor activities independently. The CCTA Total Acquisition Process (TAP) is used by many government departments when procuring products and/or services. The CCTA publication **A Guide to Procurement within the Total Acquisition Process** describes the process in detail.

8. Bibliography

Guidelines for Directing Information Systems Strategy. CCTA, 1988.

Information Systems Guide A2, Strategic Planning for Information Systems. CCTA; Published by John Wiley & Sons, Chichester 1989: ISBN 0 471 92522 5.

Information Systems Guide B6, Procurement. CCTA; Published by John Wiley & Sons, Chichester 1989: ISBN 0 471 92531 4.

A Guide to Procurement within the Total Acquisition Process. CCTA; Published by HMSO, Norwich 1991: ISBN 0 946683 58 1.

The Services Directive (Council Directive 92/50/EEC of 18 June 1992) - effective from 1 July 1993

Public Supply Contracts Regulations 1991

The Quality Management Library. CCTA; Published by CCTA, 1992: ISBN 0 11 330569 9.

Competing for Quality White Paper. CM1730; Published by HMSO, London 1991.

The PRINCE manuals published as a set by the National Computing Centre, Manchester, 1990: ISBN 1 85554 012 6.

Market Testing IS/IT Booklets are available from the Library, CCTA, Riverwalk House, 157-161 Millbank, London SW1P 4RT including:

Market Testing IS/IT Provision, 1992: ISBN 0 946683 63 8.

The *Intelligent Customer*, 1993: ISBN 0 946683 64 6.

Annex A. Glossary of Terms

Acronyms and abbreviations used in this module

BS	British Standard
CCTA	The Government Centre for Information Systems
DBMS	Database Management System
EC	European Community
EDI	Electronic Data Interchange
FM	Facilities Management
GATT	General Agreement on Tariffs and Trade
IS	Information Systems
ISO	International Organization for Standardization
IT	Information Technology
ITT	Invitation to Tender
OR	Operational Requirement
OSI	Open Systems Interconnection
PC	Personal computer
PIR	Post-Implementation Review
PRINCE	PRojects In Controlled Environments
QMS	Quality Management System
SCT	Service Control Team
SI	Systems Integration
SLA	Service Level Agreement
SSR	Statement of Service Requirements
TAP	Total Acquisition Process

Definitions

Contracting out	The process of buying-in services, which were previously provided in-house, from a third party. In IS/IT terms it encompasses concepts such as facilities management, outsourcing, turnkeys etc.

Contracts Management Database	A database which identifies and defines the different contracts and arrangements which a customer organization has with its suppliers.
Customer	Used in this module to mean an entire organization (including the business and IT Directorate) which is involved in relationships with one or more suppliers, usually involving purchases of products and services.
Downsizing	The practice of placing systems and/or applications on smaller machines than those on which they were previously installed (often associated with a move to distributed systems).
EC Journal	The Supplement to the Official Journal of the European Community.
EC Directive	Instruction issued by the Council of the European Community.
Electronic Data Interchange	The exchange of structured data in electronic form between computer systems.
End-user	Any person using an IT service.
Facilities Management	The provision of the management, operation and support of an organization's IT services and IT infrastructure activities by an external source at agreed service levels. The services are generally provided for a set time at agreed cost.
Health Check	An analysis of how effectively an organization carries out a particular activity or series of activities (used in this module in relation to the effectiveness of relationships).
Intelligent Customer	A general description applied to an organization when its culture and procedures successfully enable the planning, implementation and use of IS/IT to meet business objectives. A team is usually established to undertake the necessary activities, which:

Intelligent Customer (continued):

* knows the organization's mission, objectives, policies and critical success factors at a business level

* knows and can define the information needs of the organization, how it is obtained and used

* understands the strategic value that IS/IT gives to the organization and is able to judge its value against the cost of provision

* can develop and maintain an IS strategy, and the associated management and technical policies, to meet business requirements

	* knows why the organization has its current services and systems, how they are related, what the future requirements are, and how to define these as service specifications
	* is aware of the important IS/IT developments which may impact the organization's services
	* can measure the performance of the IS/IT provision and monitor and review relationships with the provider
	* can understand the costs, quality and value of IT systems and services, how they support the business and set budgets for IS/IT.
Internal business customer	A business area within an organization which is a customer of an IT service provider.
Invitation To Tender	An invitation sent out by a customer to suppliers asking them to bid against a specific requirement for goods and/or services.
IT Directorate	That part of an organization which has responsibility for IT strategy and standards, and controls the development and provision of IT systems and services for the organization.
IT service provider	Responsible for providing IT services to a customer base. The provider may be internal or external to the customer organization.
IT Services	That part of the IT Directorate which is responsible for providing and managing IT services to support one or more business areas within an organization.
IT Services Manager	The person with overall responsibility for IT service quality. Typically his/her peers are the Applications Development Manager and the Administration and Finance Manager, and all are responsible to the organization's Director of IT.
Market Testing	Market Testing is the process that allows in-house costs to be compared against those of the private sector based on a fair commercial comparison.
Open Systems Interconnection	A set of standard communication protocols based upon a seven layer reference model.
Operational Requirement	A document issued by a procuring organization (usually in the public sector) providing a complete statement of requirements and issued to one or more potential suppliers of equipment and services seeking proposals from the supplier(s) to meet the requirements.
Outsourcing	See *Contracting out*.

Prime contractor	A contractor who takes full responsibility for delivery of a system and/or set of services where the products and services are provided by the contractor and one or more sub-contractors.
PRINCE	The method recommended by CCTA for planning, managing and controlling IS projects. It provides guidance on the management components (organization, plans and controls) and on the technical components (end products and the activities needed to produce them).
Quality Management System	The organizational structure, responsibilities, procedures, processes and resources for implementing quality management.
Service Control Team	A team of people with skills roughly equivalent to business analysts, who are responsible for managing the relationships and contract with an external supplier (service provider), on behalf of the customer organization, when service provision has been contracted out.
Service Level Agreement	A written agreement or 'contract' between the customer of an IT service and the IT service provider which documents the agreed service levels for an IT service. Typically for an operational service it will cover: service hours, service availability, end-user support levels, throughput and terminal response times, restrictions, functionality and the service levels to be provided in a contingency. It may also include security and accounting policy.
Statement of Service Requirements	A document developed as part of the procurement process, containing a complete statement of the organization's requirements, within a specified scope, addressed to one or more possible service providers, and designed to draw from each provider a proposal describing in detail how the provider could meet the requirements.
Strategic Partnership	An agreement between two organizations to co-operate for mutual benefit and understanding of business needs and requirements - not a partnership in the legal sense.
Supplier	Any organization, external to the customer organization, currently supplying, or with the potential to supply, products or services to a customer with or without a formal contract.
Supplier Manager	A person within a customer organization who "owns" the relationship with one or more suppliers on behalf of the customer organization and is the prime contact for both supplier and internal personnel on any issues concerning the relationship.

Annex B. Supplier and customer requirements from a relationship

In every relationship between a customer and a supplier there will be a list of requirements that each party is looking to meet. These requirements can generally be met, or an acceptable compromise reached, if good relationships, backed up by good contracts as appropriate, are maintained.

B.1 A good relationship

A relationship can be defined as the mutual dealings, connections or feelings that exist between two bodies. All aspects of the relationship have to be addressed in order to get the best from it. Good relationships are built upon:

* honesty and openness

* mutual trust and respect for the capabilities of the other organization

* a desire on both sides to work together for the benefit of each other

* a mutual understanding of the goals and objectives of each other's organization

* assertiveness, not aggression, during contract negotiation (this is key because an aggressive negotiator will almost certainly win short term gains at the expense of the other organization and to the detriment of the long term relationship between the two organizations)

* enthusiasm

* attention to detail

* having customers and suppliers with a sound business knowledge of what can and cannot be compromised

* the ability of individuals to express themselves clearly and unambiguously

* good interpersonal skills

* close involvement of the decision makers within each organization.

B.2   A good contract

Not every relationship is centred around a formal contract and this module does not go into detail about how to manage contracts. This is covered in more detail in CCTA **Information Systems Guide B6, Procurement**. However, it is appropriate to list some of the elements which go into making a good contract. A good contract:

* sets out in clear and precise terms the scope of the work to which it applies

* defines clearly the roles, responsibilities, liabilities and expectations of the parties governed by the contract

* defines the procedures to be followed if a dispute arises, or any party fails to perform, and the remedies available to the parties

* is workable and acceptable to all parties

* allows the customer to achieve value for money whilst allowing the supplier to make a reasonable profit

* contains agreed and reasonable targets and performance measures

* has clearly defined change control applied

* is not unnecessarily arduous (any supplier who feels tied to an over-rigorous contract may well be tempted to cover the risk financially, possibly by reducing support costs or increasing the margin on goods or services being provided)

* is written in plain language

* clearly sets out the payment terms and conditions

* is not a stick with which to beat the other party.

Clearly the level of detail of the contract depends on the size and scale of the purchase which it covers. The type of contract is also a factor to be considered. In some cases it might be said that the customer is buying the relationship rather than a product. More detail on relationship types is given in Annex E.

B.3 What a customer wants

Customers generally look for the following in their dealings with a supplier:

* the required goods and/or services of the right quality, delivered on time and at a reasonable price

* value for money, rather than simply the best price (of course it is possible for the best price to reflect best value for money but one does not always go hand-in-hand with the other)

* the delivery of the services or goods to proceed smoothly

* a clear contact point within the supplier who has the required level of authority to be able to commit to delivery of the goods and services

* no surprises

* issues raised early

* any problem raised is accompanied by one or more potential solutions wherever possible

* a clear escalation route for resolving difficulties and as a last resort a clear disputes procedure

* not to be **locked in** to one supplier - in other words to keep their options open

* reasonable payment terms with most monies payable after delivery and acceptance of the goods and services

* suppliers to be keen to succeed for the good of the customer and not just for their own profit motives

* suppliers that understand the customer's business and IT needs

* an open and honest approach from the supplier

* respect for their business knowledge and acumen.

B.4 What a supplier wants

Suppliers generally look for the following in their dealings with a customer:

* to make a profit

* to be paid on time

* clear definition of the goods and services to be provided under the contract

* a clear definition of supplier responsibilities

* reasonable payment terms without large retentions

* a clear understanding of who the buyer is

* access to people who can help them understand more fully what is **needed** rather than what has been **specified**

* a clear escalation route for resolving difficulties and as a last resort a clear disputes procedure

* to be seen to deliver value for money and hence increase their chances of winning further business

* to be able to understand, manage and therefore meet the customer's expectations

* to create a reference site for future sales opportunities

* reasonable timeframes in which to deliver the goods and services

* to incur minimal overhead in supplying the goods or services

* no surprises

* issues raised early

* minimum exposure to risk

* constructive feedback at all levels on their performance

* an open and honest approach from the customer

* respect for their industry and business acumen.

Annex C. Checklist for reviewing current relationships

C.1   Purpose

The checklist below can serve a number of purposes. Initially it can be used to assess existing customer and supplier relationships and to identify areas which need to be improved. This will enable an improvement plan to be drawn up. Once this plan has been implemented, the checklist can be re-used at regular intervals to monitor the relationship over time. A separate checklist is used for each supplier.

The use of the checklist is discussed in Section 3.1.7.1.

C.2   The checklist

The person conducting the initial health check of the relationship (usually the Project Manager for the project set up to establish effective supplier relationships) completes the list by ticking the relevant boxes. When all checks have been made the total score is calculated by adding the individual scores in the boxes ticked. In general the higher the score the healthier the relationship. The checklist can be extended by subsequent reviewers in the light of experience.

The questions on the checklist all have 'yes' or 'no' answers. If the Project Manager is unable to establish the answer from within the organization then the answer which gives the lowest score should be ticked. If no one can provide an answer to a question then this is evidence that the Supplier Manager functions are not being addressed by the organization as a whole and that improvements can be made.

Once the project to establish effective supplier relationships is complete the Supplier Manager should use the checklist as a tool to monitor relationships at regular intervals.

No.	Question			
1	Is there a nominated Supplier Manager for the relationship?	Yes	3	Go to 2
		No	-5	Go to 8
2	Does he/she have the authority to make decisions and commit resource on behalf of the organization?	Yes	1	Go to 4
		No	-1	Go to 3
3	Does he/she have direct access to people who have this authority?	Yes	1	Go to 4
		No	-1	Go to 4
4	Is he/she from IT Services or an *intelligent customer* (see definition in Glossary)?	Yes	1	Go to 7
		No	-1	Go to 5
5	Are there plans to train the Supplier Manager?	Yes	1	Go to 6
		No	-1	Go to 6
6	Does the fact that the Supplier Manager is not from IT Services or an *intelligent customer* adversely affect the relationship?	Yes	-1	Go to 7
		No	1	Go to 7
7	Is there a nominated deputy to cover for the Supplier Manager in his/her absence?	Yes	1	Go to 8
		No	-1	Go to 8
8	Does the supplier have a single person who owns the relationship on their behalf?	Yes	3	Go to 9
		No	-5	Go to 12
9	Does he/she have the authority to make decisions and commit resource on behalf of the supplier?	Yes	1	Go to 11
		No	-1	Go to 10
10	Does he/she have direct access to people who have this authority?	Yes	1	Go to 11
		No	-1	Go to 12
11	Does he/she understand your organization and industry sector?	Yes	1	Go to 12
		No	-1	Go to 12
12	Do you feel that the relationship works for your organization?	Yes	1	Go to 13
		No	-1	Go to 13
13	Do you know how the supplier feels about the relationship?	Yes	1	Go to 14
		No	-1	Go to 15

14	Is the supplier happy with the relationship?	Yes	1	Go to 15
		No	-1	Go to 15
15	Do you hold regular meetings with the supplier?	Yes	1	Go to 16
		No	-1	Go to 17
16	Do these meetings have specific objectives which are clearly understood by both sides?	Yes	1	Go to 17
		No	-1	Go to 17
17	Are issues raised early enough to be addressed quickly and efficiently?	Yes	2	Go to 18
		No	-2	Go to 18
18	Do you get too many issues?	Yes	-2	Go to 19
		No	1	Go to 19
19	Do you pay all bills promptly?	Yes	2	Go to 22
		No	-2	Go to 20
20	Do you have to return a significant number of bills because of errors?	Yes	-1	Go to 21
		No	1	Go to 22
21	Does the supplier know how and when to present his invoices?	Yes	1	Go to 22
		No	-1	Go to 22
22	Do you trust the supplier to deliver what you want, when you want it?	Yes	1	Go to 24
		No	-1	Go to 23
23	Do you often need to resort to the contract to make the supplier perform?	Yes	-1	Go to 24
		No	1	Go to 24
24	Are you aware of new and future product offerings from the supplier?	Yes	1	Go to 25
		No	-1	Go to 25
25	Is the supplier generally aware of your product needs?	Yes	1	Go to 26
		No	-1	Go to 26
26	When you raise a problem with the supplier do you propose a solution?	Yes	1	Go to 27
		No	-1	Go to 27
27	When the supplier raises a problem with you does he/she propose a solution?	Yes	1	Go to 28
		No	-1	Go to 28

28	Do you feel in control of the relationship?	Yes	1	Go to 29
		No	-1	Go to 29
29	Are there any contacts with the supplier that you should have but do not?	Yes	-2	Go to 30
		No	1	Go to 32
30	Are you seeking to rectify this?	Yes	1	Go to 31
		No	-1	Go to 32
31	Is the supplier resisting the contact being made?	Yes	-1	Go to 32
		No	1	Go to 32
32	Is the Purchasing and Contracts Section using change control to manage changes to contracts?	Yes	1	Go to 33
		No	-1	Go to 33
33	Are there clearly understood escalation procedures on both sides?	Yes	1	END
		No	-1	END

Calculate score of relationship   [   ] Total

Date on which checklist applied   ..../......./.......

Change from last application of checklist
[ ] Pos
[ ] Neg
[ ] Nil

In addition, note the following information:

How many contracts exist with the supplier?   [   ]

Is the supplier key to the business objectives of the organization?
Yes [ ]
No [ ]

Is the supplier likely to remain/become key to the business objectives of the organization?
Yes [ ]
No [ ]

Annex D. Roles and responsibilities for supplier management

This Annex shows the roles and responsibilities of the functions within a customer organization as they relate to the customer/supplier interface. The majority of these roles fall within the IT Services area and are defined in more detail in other modules of the IT Infrastructure Library. However other functions outside of IT Services are included for completeness such as the Purchasing and Contracts Section. They are in alphabetical order for ease of reference.

It will not be appropriate in some organizations to have a different member of staff fulfilling each of these roles, and in some instances two or more roles may be merged into one. It is also likely that the roles will carry different names in some organizations. This said, the totality of management and liaison responsibilities described in the role descriptions in this Annex should be covered by an organization in some way. For further information on the structuring of IT Services organizations see the **IT Services Organization** module in the IT Infrastructure Library.

D.1 Availability Manager

The Availability Manager has a mainly management role in his dealings with suppliers. The Availability Manager typically:

* has prime responsibility for ensuring the availability of all services on a day-to-day basis and to apply corrective and preventative maintenance as required to meet the availability requirements; the four prime concerns being

  - reliability

  - serviceability

  - resilience

  - recoverability

* participates in the negotiation and management of contracts with suppliers which underpin Service Level Agreements by monitoring the compliance of suppliers to contractual conditions regarding availability

* ensures that the availability requirements of new services to be added to existing systems can be met by existing contracts

* analyzes reliability data on components serviced by suppliers, often based on data supplied by the suppliers

* tries to ensure that appropriate serviceability metrics are included in existing contracts and certainly in new contracts

* discusses with suppliers the resilience and recoverability, including disaster recovery, of their proposed system configurations

* includes suppliers in availability planning

* has a role in the forward planning and ongoing management of third party and single source maintenance contracts.

D.2 Capacity Manager

The Capacity Manager has mainly a liaison role with suppliers and typically:

* has overall responsibility for ensuring that there is adequate IT capacity to meet the required levels of service and performance by identifying when new hardware and/or software purchases are required, using information from suppliers to assist him/her in this task (this includes keeping the organization aware of relevant emerging technology)

* is the organization's technical authority on detailed issues relating to the performance of the suppliers' products

* monitors the performance of supplier systems and ensures, by working closely with suppliers, that new systems software does not cause a deterioration in performance

* selects appropriate support tools and liaises with suppliers regarding training in the use of these tools.

D.3 Change Manager

The Change Manager's role in supplier relationships is also primarily a liaison role. The Change Manager typically:

* ensures that contracts with suppliers and maintainers incorporate the requirement for the contractor's staff to comply with the organizations change management system

* liaises with suppliers, as required, to co-ordinate change building, testing and implementation to ensure that these activities are carried out to schedule

* ensures that contracts are updated to reflect agreed changes.

D.4 Computer Operations Manager

The Computer Operations Manager, when dealing with suppliers, has a mainly liaison role. In some instances he/she will have the authority to insist that supplier staff adhere to instructions (especially on security, and health and safety matters) and could have management responsibility for third party and single source maintainers. The Computer Operations Manager typically:

* plans and oversees the installation and acceptance of computer hardware from suppliers

* ensures that the physical environment is maintained and secure according to contractual and organizational requirements

* ensures that new production systems meet the agreed operability criteria for live running prior to acceptance from suppliers

* ensures that all contractual documentation for incidents in the Operations domain is complete

* has a role in the ongoing management of third party and single source maintainers

* ensures that Health and Safety regulations concerning the operations area are taken into account when dealing with suppliers, and that the suppliers comply as required

* meets regularly with site engineers to ensure maintenance schedules are adhered to

* contributes to decision making on the purchase of hardware to support service level requirements

* ensures that engineers have adequate facilities on site

* liaises with suppliers on tools requirements.

D.5 Contingency Planning Manager

Essentially a liaison role the Contingency Planning Manager typically:

* works with suppliers in the production of contingency plans and arranges and monitors tests of these plans

* is responsible for the placement of the underpinning contracts

* assists the procurement officer in the negotiation of 'dormant' contracts for the supply of hardware in the event of a disaster befalling an organization

* regularly reviews 'dormant' and other contracts in which he/she has an interest.

D.6 End-users

End-users may from time to time have contact with service engineers and in certain circumstances need to contact a supplier's Help Desk. Through User Groups, end-users may also meet with suppliers to pass on requirements, ideas, suggestions etc and to learn of new developments and plans. End-users have no management role in the customer and supplier relationship.

D.7 Help Desk

The customer Help Desk function rarely carries management authority. Where there is an element of supplier management it is typically only ensuring that suppliers meet call out and incident resolution targets and provide any reports as set out in a contract. Typically the Help Desk:

* provides information on the performance of suppliers' products and engineers

* calls upon suppliers to provide direct support in incident investigation and diagnosis - with other suppliers' personnel if necessary on a multi-supplier site

* liaises with suppliers to assist in the forecasting of future demands on the Help Desk and the monitoring techniques best suited to the environment.

D.8 IT Security Officer

The IT Security Officer plays both a management and liaison role. The management aspects relate generally to security issues when suppliers' staff are working on the organizations premises. Typically, the IT Security Officer:

* provides a central point of contact on IT security within the organization for both internal staff and external suppliers

* co-ordinates security relating to shared IT infrastructures

* advises the Procurement Officer and Purchasing and Contract Section as to what security requirements to include in ORs, SSRs and contracts

* receives reports on IT security incidents from both internal staff and external suppliers and co-ordinates action where required

* ensures that suppliers' staff comply with and are subject to the relevant security arrangements for access to site, buildings, rooms, data etc.

D.9 IT Senior management

Senior management, such as the IT Director, must demonstrate their commitment to any project to improve the quality of customer and supplier relationships if any such project is to provide lasting benefit. This has been addressed in Section 3.2.1.

In their dealings with suppliers, the senior management role is essentially one of liaison although any escalation procedures are likely to involve senior managers as the second level of escalation. Typically, senior management establish and maintain a rapport with their peers in the supplier organization and this is to be actively encouraged. The agenda for this contact should be as wide reaching as possible unless there are specific items to address.

D.10 Manager for Local Processors and Terminals

The Manager for Local Processors and Terminals has little contact with suppliers and has essentially a liaison role, typically he/she:

* keeps up to date with the technology by liaison with suppliers

* deals with the delivery, installation, acceptance, maintenance and repair of equipment, through local Systems Administrators as appropriate

* provides a degree of central co-ordination of the local infrastructure.

D.11 Network Services Manager

The Network Services Manager has specific management responsibility when dealing with suppliers. It is common for network components and services to be provided by a different number of suppliers and the Network Services Manager must negotiate contracts, monitor the performance of suppliers' products and services against contractual conditions, and manage the relationships with those suppliers to ensure the quality of network services is maintained.

D.12 Operational Test Manager

The Operational Test Manager role is essentially one of liaison with suppliers although when both user and supplier organizations have acceptance test teams it is the Operational Test Manager's responsibility to resolve any conflict between these teams. The Operational Test Manager typically:

* liaises with suppliers during installation and acceptance testing

* liaises with in-house acceptance test teams

* assesses techniques and tools for automating operational testing.

D.13 Payments unit

Payments unit receives, logs and arranges for invoices to be checked before payment is made. Where invoices are inaccurate, Payments unit liaise with the supplier in an attempt to resolve any issues. Should resolution prove impossible the matter should be referred to the Supplier Manager. Where invoices are accurate and due for payment, Payments unit arranges for payment to be made.

D.14 Problem Manager

The Problem Manager's role is primarily one of liaison with the suppliers. The Problem Manager typically:

* provides an effective interface between the IT Directorate and suppliers in relation to problems, including resolution statistics, regular reports and reviews

* reports security incidents involving suppliers to the IT Security Officer

* includes suppliers' staff who regularly attend or support the site in training in, and acceptance of, the in-house problem management system

* sets up functional supplier groups within the problem management function where there is a large multi-supplier environment

* handles potential disputes between suppliers in multi-supplier environments

* makes suppliers aware of the management information which is produced from the in-house PM system and is then used to monitor performance against contracts

* has responsibility for ensuring that the supplier's problem management system interfaces with that of his/her own organization

* makes use of suppliers' engineering reports to identify potential problems before they occur.

D.15 Procurement Officer

Essentially a liaison role, the post is normally located in a Purchasing and Contracts Section (see D.16), and the Procurement Officer typically:

* arranges the purchase of new hardware, software, communications equipment, services, consultancy etc

* assists in preparing Operational Requirements (ORs) or Statement of Service Requirements (SSRs)

* issues the OR or SSR, assesses responses, arranges discussions and demonstrations as appropriate

* assists in drafting contracts and the final selection of the successful supplier

* implements management's procurement policy on issues such as preferred suppliers, standard packages, standard operating systems, communications etc.

D.16 Purchasing and Contracts Section

A Purchasing and Contracts Section typically:

* manages the procurement of supplies and services - see D.15 for the role of the Procurement Officer

* ensures that an organization's business requirements are clearly and unambiguously stated in the contract

* negotiates the terms and conditions of contracts with suppliers

* drafts the contract (or reviews the supplier's drafts) and variations to the contract

* ensures that the organization's interests are not compromised by any contract it enters into

* either carries final authority to sign off variations to the contracts or is an essential part of the sign-off process, depending upon the structure of the organization

* initiates the process of seeking legal remedy from suppliers should the need arise

* carries out contract reviews.

D.17 Service Control Team

The Service Control Team (SCT) is the usual interface between an organization and an FM supplier/external service provider and the role is essentially a management one. The SCT typically:

*   interfaces with the supplier during the planning of the handover of service provision and oversees the ongoing management of the service contract

*   has responsibility for the technical management and auditing of the service contract.

The SCT is part of the intelligent customer function within the customer organization.

D.18 Service Level Manager

The Service Level Manager liaises with suppliers but does not usually have management authority. The Service Level Manager typically:

*   reviews existing underpinning supply and maintenance contracts

*   ensures that new contracts are negotiated as necessary (by the Availability Manager) which are capable of supporting the service levels set out in the Service Level Agreements with internal customers.

D.19 Supplier Manager

The Supplier Manager role is the key management role in the customer and supplier relationship. The need for one or more Supplier Managers and the responsibilities of the role(s) will vary according to the size of the organization. One Supplier Manager may cover all relationships with a single supplier, a number of suppliers in a single project, or with several suppliers for all the dealings with those suppliers. The Supplier Manager typically:

*   'owns' the relationship on behalf of the customer organization

*   is a catalyst which enables the two organizations to work together to the benefit of both

*   regularly monitors the contacts between the two organizations to ensure that they are at the right level and conducted properly

* ensures that internal communications, relating to suppliers, are effective and efficient

* canvasses the views of staff within his/her organization on supplier performance and reports to senior management

* assists the Purchasing and Contracts Section in drawing up contracts with supplier(s)

* is involved in the sign-off of all changes to contracts with supplier(s) (in many cases the Supplier Manager may well carry the final authorization for agreeing contract changes)

* is responsible for arbitrating in situations where suppliers are getting conflicting information from the customer

* is the first point of escalation for any issues or problems raised by the supplier

* visits suppliers' premises to establish and maintain visibility within that supplier

* checks invoices from suppliers to establish whether they are valid for payment (in many cases the Supplier Manager will find it more cost effective to delegate this task but must retain overall responsibility for invoice clearance).

Annex E. Typical customer and supplier relationships

There are many customer and supplier relationships, and at any one time a customer is likely to be involved in a number of these with one or more suppliers. There are two basic kinds of relationships (purchasing and non-purchasing) and it is possible for the relationship between a customer and supplier to move from one kind to another over a period of time (an informal meeting with a supplier identifies a common interest which may lead to that supplier successfully bidding for work).

It is also possible for a supplier to move from one type of purchasing relationship to another (for example a supplier may be chosen through competitive tender for one requirement but may then win further business through a single tender process).

Figure E1 shows the main types of relationships both purchasing and non-purchasing.

Figure E1: The main types of customer and supplier relationships

Purchasing	Non-Purchasing
One-off purchase	Informal
Single tender purchase	Formal
Competitive tender purchase	Strategic
Call-off contract	
Fixed price contract	
Enabling arrangement	
Prime contractor/ turnkey contract	
Strategic partnership	
Consortia	

E.1 Purchasing relationships

These may be linked with one or more contracts. There are many purchasing relationships. The list below is not comprehensive, but it does represent some of the more common types.

E.1.1 One-off purchase

This can cover the purchase of goods or services but more generally this type of relationship will be seen when an organization is buying a specific product (PC, software package, printer etc), usually a proprietary item, against a well defined need. This can often be achieved by use of a simple purchase order. In many cases the contact with the supplier will be minimal and the need to invest time in building a good relationship need go no further than to conduct business in a professional manner.

Where an ongoing maintenance or support arrangement is required the relationship moves to one of the other types such as fixed price contract (E.1.5) or call-off contract (E.1.4).

E.1.2 Single tender purchase

This can cover the purchase of high value goods and services as well as lower value items. As a purchasing option it is most likely to be used when the organization has a good knowledge of the potential supplier and/or their product, or when there are no equivalent products or services available from other sources. In the past this could be due to an organization being locked into one supplier of computing equipment but this is now less likely since the move towards open systems and multi-supplier architectures.

One advantage of the single tender purchase is that there is no need to evaluate several tenders from different suppliers. The major disadvantage is the greater difficulty in ensuring value for money is achieved.

If an organization chooses to use the single tender route the implication is that it already has a relationship with the chosen supplier.

Public bodies are subject to EC/GATT legislation on procurement and can only use the single tender option in clearly defined circumstances. More information on this aspect can be obtained from the CCTA.

E.1.3 Competitive tender purchase

This is seen by many as the best way to ensure value for money from suppliers and is frequently used for all but low value, low risk purchases. Indeed, many organizations will, as a result of government and EC/GATT legislation, be required to use competitive tender unless they meet certain exception criteria.

For other than specific commodity purchases customers must define clearly their requirements for goods or services, either in an OR or an SSR to enable suppliers to propose the most appropriate goods or services of the type or quality required. A customer must also have a clear view of how it will judge the responses when it receives them, ie clearly defined evaluation criteria.

Customers not covered by EC/GATT legislation should resist the temptation to issue an ITT to many suppliers when they already have a firm idea of which are most likely to provide the required goods and/or services. Responding to an ITT may take a significant amount of time and effort on a supplier's part and if it is seen that this is going to be wasted then a supplier is less likely to bid for further business.

E.1.4 Call-off contract

This can be used when the organization knows what goods or services it requires from a supplier but does not have a clear view of when it wants the goods or services to be provided. The contract will have agreed costs for the goods and/or services up to a maximum value and usually a maximum duration (for example the supply and installation of up to 500 PCs over three years, or agreed call out charge and hourly rates for service engineers).

E.1.5 Fixed price contract

With this type of contract the price (and usually the duration) is agreed at the outset either for the duration of the contract or a set period, ie 12 months, but with a fixed method of calculating increases. If a supplier can reduce costs and/or finish early then this is likely to increase the profit from the contract. Delays and slippage will reduce the profit. The advantage for an organization letting a fixed price contract is that the cost is known at the outset. However, suppliers may well cover any risk of slipping by quoting higher prices, although the risk is greatly reduced in a competitive tendering situation.

This type of approach is best used when the requirement is well defined and the likelihood of change is small.

Maintenance contracts are typically fixed price but in these cases the comments above regarding early finish, reduced costs (to some degree) and slippage would not apply.

E.1.6 Enabling Arrangement

This type of relationship allows a customer and a supplier to agree terms and conditions, unit prices for items and/or services (these can be in ranges rather than exact prices) which will apply should the supplier be contracted to provide goods or service to that organization. Although the customer has no legal obligation to place work with the supplier there is an implied intention on the part of the customer to pass a regular supply of work to the supplier. The rates are usually fixed each year with increases agreed between each party. This type of relationship considerably reduces the amount of effort required when setting up a contract should work be let.

An organization may have enabling arrangements with several preferred suppliers who have been selected on a competitive basis.

E.1.7 Prime contractor/ turnkey contract

These types of contract are suitable for the more complex tasks where more than one supplier is likely to be involved. Whilst the terms are often interchanged there is a difference in these contracts.

In a prime contractor situation there is always more than one contractor involved. One supplier may be able to provide the major part of the solution, and thereby act as prime contractor, but requires the input of one or more sub-contractors to provide the total package.

In a turnkey contract, one supplier is contracted to provide a total solution and may be able to provide the entire solution themselves but will often use sub-contractors.

In either case the customer looks upon the prime contractor or turnkey supplier to take managerial responsibility for delivery of the total solution. However in strict contractual terms turnkey relationships imply that the main supplier is financially accountable for the performance of any sub-contractors used and this is not necessarily the case with the prime contractor situation.

E.1.8 Strategic partnership

Strategic partnerships are typically set up when an organization's business and IS strategy has defined a reliance on the goods and/or services of a supplier over a significant time frame. This reliance will typically go beyond individual projects.

Strategic partnerships are not partnerships in the legal sense but an agreement to co-operate for mutual benefit and understanding of business needs and requirements. A strategic partnership may encompass a combination of the other arrangements referred to in this Annex.

Within the public sector and in some industry sectors, such as Utilities, EC legislation requires that fair competition is not compromised and this may well rule out the use of this type of relationship.

E.1.9 Consortia

Consortia are generally formed to meet a diverse set of requirements from a customer where no one member of the consortium can provide the total solution. Consortia can be established by the suppliers themselves or at the specific request of a customer. Generally one member of the consortia will act as prime contractor.

It is possible for consortia to be set up to address any of the relationship types given in E.1.1 to E.1.8 above.

E.2 Non-purchasing relationships

These are regarded as falling into three basic types.

E.2.1 Informal

These can be at any level in an organization. Typically they cover the requesting of literature, attendance at presentations and workshops and similar activities. The information flow tends to be more from the supplier to a customer and no formal management of the relationship is required.

E.2.2 Formal

These tend to start at middle management level. Typically these contacts would encompass formal meetings and updates on supplier developments and customer requirements.

The information flow is two-way and the relationship does need to be managed effectively. It is common for a purchasing relationship to evolve from this type of contact.

There may also be a formal relationship between a customer and supplier, based on a written agreement but not a formal contract, for example to jointly develop a product.

E.2.3 Strategic

These will generally be at senior management level. Typically these contacts will involve discussions of strategic issues and future developments and will seek to find common visions and goals. These relationships may be the foundation for future risk-sharing developments in commercial organizations.

Annex F. Interfaces between customer and supplier organizations

The number of possible interfaces between customer and supplier organizations are many and varied. Figure F1 shows the most common interfaces within a customer and supplier relationship in a matrix format, but these may vary from organization to organization. The emphasis within the customer organization is on roles within IT Services, although some other associated roles are also included.

CUSTOMER ORGANIZATION	SUPPLIER ORGANIZATION									
	SM	CAM	SAM	LC	IS	PM	IE	SEM	HD	ME
Availability Manager	-	X	-	-	-	-	-	X	X	X
Capacity Manager	X	X	X	-	-	X	-	X	-	-
Change Manager	-	-	-	-	-	-	-	X	-	-
Computer Operations Manager	-	X	X	-	-	X	X	X	-	X
Contingency Planning Manager	-	X	X	-	-	-	-	-	-	-
End-users	-	-	-	-	-	-	-	-	X	X
Help Desk	-	-	-	-	-	-	-	X	X	X
IT Security Officer	-	X	-	X	-	-	X	-	-	X
IT senior management	X	X	-	-	-	-	-	-	-	-
Manager of Local Procs & Terms	-	-	X	-	-	-	-	-	-	-
Network Services Manager	-	-	-	-	-	-	-	X	-	X
Operational Test Manager	-	-	-	-	-	-	X	X	-	-
Payments unit	-	X	-	-	X	-	-	-	-	-
Problem Manager	-	-	-	-	-	-	-	X	X	X
Procurement Officer	-	X	X	X	-	-	-	-	-	-
Purchasing and Contracts	-	X	X	X	-	-	-	-	-	-
Service Control Team	-	-	-	-	-	-	-	X	X	-
Service Level Manager	-	-	-	-	-	-	-	X	-	-
Supplier Manager	X	X	X	X	X	X	-	X	X	-

KEY

SM	-	Senior management	SEM	-	Service Manager
PM	-	Production Manager	LC	-	Legal and Contracts staff
CAM	-	Customer Account Manager	HD	-	Help Desk staff
IE	-	Installation engineers	IS	-	Invoicing section
SAM	-	Sales Manager	ME	-	Maintenance engineers

Figure F1: Possible interfaces between a customer and a supplier

It can be seen from the matrix that the customer generally has a higher number of roles involved in the relationship than the supplier, although in many organizations, especially small customer organizations, roles will be combined and the number of people involved may be considerably less.

Relationships in general are likely to be more effective when there are fewer contact points to maintain and organizations should review the number and frequency of their contacts with a view to reducing them to a minimum. It is essential that the communication paths within each organization are efficient and effective.

Annex G. Methods for updating contracts

Often problems can be caused by contracts being allowed to get out of step with agreed changes. Having formal change control on contracts ensures that any changes are agreed by all parties but the benefit that this brings can be lost if the contracts are not then updated to reflect the new agreement. The **Change Management** module of the IT Infrastructure Library provides guidance on establishing and managing a change management function.

Many methods can be used to update contracts and both the size of the contract (in financial terms, in duration or in the complexity of the job of work to which it relates) and the complexity of the change, will have a bearing on deciding which is the most appropriate.

It must also be remembered that variations can be for an increase or decrease in the scope of a contract. Either way it is vital to ensure that contracts are updated in a timely and effective manner.

The following sections describe three methods:

* letter (G.1)

* revised wording with covering letter (G.2)

* replacement pages with covering letter (G.3).

For each of the above methods certain important details must be included in the letter or covering letter, and these are:

* the contract reference

* the change reference (or any other unique reference by which the change can be identified)

* the agreed costs of the change (in some cases this may be a written quote from the supplier which the customer has accepted in which case reference must be made to the quotation number)

* instructions on how the supplier signifies acceptance of the change (see section G.4 below)

* any special instructions on how the supplier is to invoice against the change (see section G.5 below).

G.1 Letter

A letter from a customer to the supplier setting out clearly and unambiguously the terms of the agreed change will often suffice if the variation is of a minor nature and/or the contract is of low value, short term or relatively simple. This is the least comprehensive way in which the contract can be updated.

G.2 Revised wording with covering letter

This is more suitable for medium sized contracts. It relies upon a customer and supplier each revising the wording of their contract in accordance with instructions given in the covering letter which is sent to the supplier once a change has been agreed.

Whilst more comprehensive than the letter approach at G.1, this still requires both customer and supplier to have the internal disciplines to ensure that the wording is changed. The main advantage of this method over the method at G.1, is that the variations are reflected in the contractual document rather than as a series of letters which are filed with (and may well get separated from) the original document.

In this case the covering letter must also include the following details:

*   a brief description of the change to which the letter refers

*   clear and unambiguous instructions on which text within the contract needs to be amended and the new text that is to be inserted (detailed checks must be made to ensure that the textual changes reflect exactly the agreed change).

G.3 Replacement pages with covering letter

This method is the most comprehensive but can also be the most costly on an organization's resources since new pages have to be produced for every part of the contract which is affected by each agreed change. It is the recommended method for any contracts of significance where a government department is the customer.

This method, which is most appropriate for the longer term and more complex contracts, requires the contract to be in a form where pages can be replaced. It can be used to equal effect on small and medium sized contracts but a judgement needs to be made as to whether the extra effort on the organization's part is justified by the benefits over the other methods described above.

There are many advantages of this method. The main one is that the effort required to update the contract, once the pages have been produced, is minimal. It also allows previous revisions to be kept for audit purposes.

With this method the covering letter must also contain the following details:

* a brief description of the change which is the subject of the letter

* clear and unambiguous instructions on which pages are to be replaced and where to insert any new pages.

In addition, each replacement page also must include:

* the contract reference

* the change reference (or any other unique reference by which the change can be identified)

* the date on which the page was issued.

G.4 Supplier acceptance

Whichever method is chosen to update the contract there must be a mechanism by which the supplier signifies his acceptance of the change and which provides him with the opportunity to seek clarification or point out errors.

The simplest way in which a supplier signifies acceptance of a variation is to return a copy of the covering letter, duly signed by an authorized person within that supplier.

A more rigorous approach can be used when replacement pages are used. This requires authorized representatives of both the customer and the supplier to sign each page before it is accepted as an agreed change to the contract. This method does allow areas of concern to be identified more quickly and dealt with in isolation from amendments which are acceptable to both parties.

G.5 Supplier invoicing against changes

Depending upon the nature of the contract, suppliers can invoice for changes in a number of ways. Two are most commonly used.

For supply of goods such as hardware, software, communications equipment etc, it is often more appropriate to invoice separately for each change. For example if a change is agreed to increase the number of workstations by five units, than an invoice for those five units can be issued separately.

For supply of services it may not be as easy to break out each change and invoicing may continue as before but to a revised total figure.

Irrespective of how the invoices are presented, the change reference should be included by the supplier on any invoice which covers work covered by one or more agreed changes.

G.6 Tracking changes

The longer and more complex the work covered by a contract, the more likely it is that changes will occur. These need to be tracked.

By far the best way to do this is to have a schedule in the contract specifically for tracking changes. This schedule should cross refer to the approval of the changes under the change management system. An example of a format which can be used for this purpose is given in Figure G1.

	RECORD OF AUTHORIZED AMENDMENTS TO CONTRACTS		
Revision No	Detail of change	Date Rev. Issued	New Pages
REV1	Detailed under Change Control Reference 1/92 This change details the addition of new hardware in the Phase 1 equipment list	30/4/92	5 51, 52 53, 54 77
REV2	Detailed under Change Control Reference 3/92 This change redefines the service levels to be achieved on the system	26/8/92	5 51, 52 53, 53a 55 77
REV3	Etc		
Figure G1: Tracking contract variations			

Annex H. Qualities and skills for managing relationships

Certain qualities and skills are desirable in personnel who are involved in managing supplier relationships. The greater the involvement the more importance the qualities and skills assume. The Supplier Manager in particular needs to have many of the following:

* acceptability - a personal style which enables them to get on well with colleagues, or suppliers

* adaptability - the ability to maintain effectiveness with changing environments, tasks, responsibilities or people

* assertiveness - the ability to be positive and decisive in discussions without being aggressive

* controlled response - the ability to remain calm and objective when confronted with difficult situations

* interpersonal sensitivity - an awareness of the feelings and needs of other people

* logical thinking - the ability to reach logical decisions using an unbiased, rational approach

* judgement - the ability to make a reasoned, balanced assessment of a situation

* objectivity - the ability to remain objective and fair in discussions and not become over-emotional

* oral communication - effectiveness of expression in individual or group situations

* organizational sensitivity - the ability to perceive the impact and implications of decisions and activities on other parts of an organization (either their own or suppliers)

* persuasiveness - the ability to present ideas and facts in a convincing manner and to convince others of a particular viewpoint; able to obtain agreement or acceptance of plans

* problem analysis - the ability to identify problems, seek relevant data, recognise important information and to diagnose the possible causes of problems

* rapport building - the ability to approach and mix easily with other people

* team contributor - a willingness to participate as a full member of a group of which they are not necessarily leader; an effective contributor even when the group is working on something of no direct personal interest

* written communication - the ability to express ideas clearly in unambiguous terms.

CCTA hopes that you find this book both useful and interesting. We will welcome your comments and suggestions for improving it.
Please use this form or a photocopy, and continue on a further sheet if needed.

From:

Name

Organization

Address

Telephone

COVERAGE
Does the material cover your needs?
If not, then what additional material would you like included.

CLARITY
Are there any points which are unclear?
If yes, please detail where and why.

ACCURACY
Please give details of any inaccuracies found.

If more space is required for these or other comments, please continue overleaf.

OTHER COMMENTS

Return to: **Information Systems Engineering Group**
CCTA,
Rosebery Court
St Andrews Business Park
Norwich NR7 0HS

Further information

Further information on the contents of this module can be obtained from:

Information Systems Engineering Group
CCTA
Rosebery Court
St Andrews Business Park
Norwich
NR7 0HS

Telephone: 01603 704704
(GTN: 3040 4704)

Printed in the United Kingdom for The Stationery Office
J72983 2/99 C3 10170